KETOGENIC

DIET

120 MOUTHWATERING MEALS

KETOGENIC DIET

120 MOUTHWATERING MEALS

1 MONTH OF LOW-CARB, HIGH-FAT WEIGHT LOSS MEALS

Recipes365

• BEFORE YOU BEGIN •

Free Bonus Guide:

Top 10 Ketogenic Diet Mistakes

We've put together a free companion guide to go with this recipe book. It features the top 10 mistakes made by people on the ketogenic diet.

If you want to avoid costly mistakes and accelerate your progress you will find a link below to get it below now!

Visit www.litomedia.com/ketogenic-mistakes to get your free bonus guide!

Table of Contents

Breakfasts

Lunches

Dinners

Desserts

INTRODUCTION

Welcome to the world's most effective high-fat, low-carb diet! By now you are probably well aware of the benefits of going keto, but just in case you need to refresh your memory here's a quick top-up before we dive into the recipes.

THE SCIENCE IN A NUTSHELL

Your body normally converts carbohydrates into glucose for energy. By limiting your intake and replacing it with fats, your body enters a state of ketosis.

Here your body produces ketones, created by a breakdown of fats in the liver. Without carbohydrates as your primary source of energy your body will turn to the ketones instead.

This effectively cranks up the fat burning furnace and puts your body in the ultimate metabolic state.

WHAT KETO CAN DO FOR YOU

Keto has its origins in treating healthcare conditions such as epilepsy, diabetes, cardiovascular disease, metabolic syndrome, auto-brewery syndrome and high blood pressure but now has much wider application in weight control.

This diet, then, will take you above and beyond typical results and propel you into a new realm of total body health. If you want to look and feel the best you possibly can, all without sacrificing your love of delicious food, then this is the cookbook for you.

THINGS TO REMEMBER

A good diet is not solution to anything in and of itself; it must be applied as part of a healthy lifestyle in order to see maximum results.

Think of the ketogenic diet as the foundation for your new body. If you want to build something truly special on top of it then design your lifestyle with that goal in mind.

Cutting out junk food goes without saying, as does ditching bad habits such as smoking and drinking. Exercise, too, will take you to heights you never knew were possible.

So, as you explore these delectable dishes and embark on the keto diet, try not to neglect other areas or responsibility.

We recommend getting some professional advice from a physician prior to commencing, since they will be able to advise you much better on your own individual goals.

With that said, we just know you will love every bite of what's to come. Don't forget to share the love and tell a friend. Having them with you on this journey will be incredibly motivational.

This is the start of something great. Let's go!

THE RECIPES

We wanted to make it as simple as possible for you to get in the kitchen and rustle up something special, so you will find each recipe laid out in an easy to follow format.

Each begins with a short intro to the dish, followed by the serving size and list of ingredients. Remember, this diet is designed to rekindle your love of food, not extinguish it with rules and regulations, so don't be afraid to experiment.

Use the ingredients as general guidelines and follow the instructions as best you can. You may not get everything perfect first time, every time, but that is what makes it yours!

Cooking and eating shouldn't be about presentation, so you won't find any fancy pictures here. In fact, you won't find any pictures at all, because they will just distract you from your goals.

When you obsess over replicating recipes to the exact photographic standards of a professional chef it becomes an impossible task. Instead, simply follow the recipes and find your own rhythm. Soon enough, you'll have created your own signature dishes!

Each recipe ends with a breakdown of key nutritional information including number of calories and amount of fats, carbohydrates and protein.

Again, this isn't to be obsessed over. Food is something to be enjoyed, so don't go trying to calculate your macros to four decimal points! Be responsible when monitoring your progress, but be reasonable, too.

Once you start loving what you are eating mealtimes will become something to look forward to, and that's when the magic happens.

So without further ado, go forth, and cook to your heart's content!

"Eating is not merely a material pleasure. Eating well gives a spectacular joy to life and contributes immensely to goodwill and happy companionship. It is of great importance to the morale."

-Elsa Schiaparelli

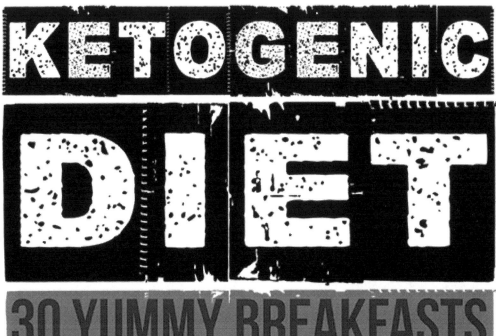

30 YUMMY BREAKFASTS

1 MONTH OF LOW-CARB, HIGH-FAT WEIGHT LOSS MEALS

Recipes365

KETO PIZZA STYLE WAFFLES

Who says you can't have dinner for breakfast? Or better yet, pizza for breakfast! And the icing on the cake (or should we say the cheese on the crust?) is that this recipe is perfect for your keto diet and gloriously customizable with your own toppings. Let's get started.

SERVING SIZE:

This recipe will produce 2 waffles.

INGREDIENTS:

1 tbsp. butter (or bacon grease)

1 tsp. baking powder

3 tbsp. almond flour

1 tsp. Italian seasoning

1 tbsp. psyllium husk powder

4 tbsp. parmesan cheese

3 oz. cheddar cheese

4 large eggs

½ cup tomato sauce

14 pepperoni slices (If you're aiming for a classic pizza)

Salt and pepper to taste

DIRECTIONS:

1. Add everything except your sauce, cheeses, and toppings to an immersion blender and mix together until thick and free of clumps.

2. Heat your waffle iron and add half your blended mixture. Many waffle irons have a handy little light that will tell you when it's ready but if not, look for the flow of steam coming from the iron to almost disappear to indicate it is ready.

3. Repeat step 3 with the rest of your mixture.

4. Add half your tomato sauce (1/4 cup) and half your cheese (1.5 oz.) to each pizza waffle.

5. Add your pepperoni, or any other toppings, to the pizzas.

6. Broil for a few minutes until the cheese begins to bubble and crisp. For cheddar, broiling generally takes about 3-5 minutes, but this time will vary with other cheese so keep an eye on it!

And there you go, two delicious pizza waffles for breakfast. Now go and have a great day!

NUTRITIONAL INFORMATION (PER SERVING):

Calories: 525

Fat: 41.5g

Carbs: 5g

Protein: 29g

MORNING MUFFINS

Waking up to a chocolate brownie craving can be such a let down. You've got your whole day ahead of you, but must restrain yourself from the delectable chocolate that's calling your name. No more! This easy chocolate morning muffin recipe will satisfy your sweet tooth while the addition of pumpkin keeps your keto diet on track.

SERVING SIZE:

This recipe will yield 6 muffins.

Ingredients:

1 tsp. vanilla extract

2 tbsp. coconut oil

½ tsp. salt

½ tsp. baking powder

1 tbsp. cinnamon

¼ cup cocoa power

1 tsp. apple cider vinegar

¼ cup slivered almonds

½ cup pumpkin puree

1 large egg

1 cup golden flaxseed meal

¼ cup sugar-free caramel syrup

DIRECTIONS:

1. Set your oven to 350°F.

2. Combine all your wet ingredients in one bowl and mix well. Do the same to your dry ingredients in a separate bowl.

3. Now pour your wet ingredients into the dry and mix. Pour slowly and be sure to mix well in order to prevent clumping.

4. Set 6 standard paper liners into your muffin tin, and add roughly ¼ cup of your mixture to each liner.

5. Sprinkle the almond slivers over the tops of the muffins for a little garnish and crunch (a dramatic flair while sprinkling is optional).

6. Bake the muffins for 15 minutes, and check. Once the muffins rise and are set then you'll know they're ready.

That's all there is to it! Quick, easy, and your sweet tooth will thank you.

NUTRITIONAL INFORMATION (PER SERVING)

Calories: 185g

Fat: 13g

Carbs: 3.5g

Protein: 7.5g

KETO WAFFLES WITH PUMPKIN SPICE

On the keto diet, it's easy to miss our favorite sweet breakfasts. Gazing at a waffle with a sense of longing or grudgingly eyeing someone while they demolish a stack of pancakes is no fun at all. But there is hope for sticking to your diet and enjoying these tasty breakfasts, with the added benefit of pumpkin!

SERVING SIZE:

This recipe will yield 2 servings.

INGREDIENTS:

1 tsp. baking powder

1 tsp. vanilla extract

3 tbsp. swerve sweetener

1 ½ tsp. pumpkin pie spice

1/3 cup coconut milk

½ cup almond flour

2 tbsp. flaxseed meal

¼ cup canned pumpkin

2 large eggs

7 drops liquid stevia

DIRECTIONS:

1. Mix all your wet ingredients in a large bowl. Be sure to mix well until no egg whites are visible.

2. Combine all dry ingredients in a sifter.

3. Sift all dry ingredients into the wet ingredients and mix as you go. If you don't have a sifter, simply mixing all the dry ingredients in a bowl and slowly sprinkling them into the wet ingredients will work too.

1. Mix the wet and dry ingredients until they are fully combined. Your mixture will be a little watery, but don't worry!

4. Heat your waffle iron and grease. Coconut spray gives your waffles a fantastic hint of coconut!

5. Pour your mixture into the iron and cook until the built in alarm goes off, or the stream of steam begins to dissipate.

Serve 'em up with your favorite syrup or fruit!

NUTRITIONAL INFORMATION (PER SERVING):

Calories: 290

Fat: 25g

Carbs: 5g

Protein: 14g

KETO CHEESE TACOS

Here we have a refreshing, and quite delectable, take on the traditional taco. Instead of fretting over the flour and carbs used in tortillas, just make your own out of cheese! That's right; eggs, avocado, and bacon wrapped in a crunchy cheese tortilla resulting in the perfect keto friendly start to your day.

SERVING SIZE:

This recipe will yield 3 servings.

INGREDIENTS:

3 strips bacon

1 oz. cheddar cheese (shredded)

1/2 avocado

2 tbsp. butter

1 cup mozzarella cheese (shredded)

6 large eggs

Salt and pepper to taste

DIRECTIONS:

1. Start by fully cooking the bacon. Either in an oven for 15 to 20 minutes at 375°F or stovetop.

2. Heat a clean pan on medium heat, and add 1/3 cup of mozzarella.

3. Heat the cheese until it just begins to bubble and turn brown on the side touching the pan. Pay close attention here! It will only take a few seconds for the cheese to jump from brown to burned.

4. Slip a spatula under the cheese and gently unstick it from the pan.

5. Now use a pair of tongs and drape the cheese over a wooden spoon, that should be resting over a bowl or pot. Allow the cheese to cool and form a taco shell shape.

6. Repeat steps 2 to 5 with the rest of your mozzarella.

7. Now add your butter and eggs to the pan and cook completely, adding salt and pepper to suit your taste.

8. Divide the eggs equally between your cheese shells.

9. Slice the avocado and divide the slices evenly between the tacos.

10. Chop or crumble your bacon, and again divide equally between the tacos.

11. Last step! Sprinkle your cheddar cheese over the tops.

All done!

NUTRITIONAL INFORMATION (PER SERVING):

Calories: 445

Fat: 36g

Carbs: 4g

Protein: 26g

KETO DONUTS

On the keto diet, resisting the pleasure of a staple comfort breakfast food can be a tearful experience. We're of course referring to donuts, but there's hope! Enter the Keto Mini Doughnuts, and those tears of sorrow may flip to joy as you bake these egg, almond, and coconut filled beauties.

SERVING SIZE:

This recipe yields 22 servings (one donut per serving).

INGREDIENTS:

4 tbsp. almond flour

1 tbsp. coconut flour

1 tsp. vanilla extract

1 tsp. baking powder

4 tbsp. erythritol

3 oz. cream cheese

3 large eggs

10 drops liquid stevia

DIRECTIONS:

1. Add all of your ingredients to a bowl or pitcher and combine with an immersion blender. A food processor will also work for this step if you don't have an immersion blender.

2. Make sure that all your ingredients are well blended and smooth.

3. Heat your donut maker and spray with your grease of choice. Coconut oil always gives your cooking a savory finish!

4. Pour your mixture into the donut maker. Don't fill all the way to the top, leave some room (say 10%) to give your donuts space to rise.

5. Let the mixture cook for 3 minutes, and then flip and cook a further 2 minutes.

6. Remove the cooked donuts and repeat steps 3 to 5 for the rest of your batter.

Voilà! You've just created 22 delicious keto friendly donuts.

NUTRITIONAL INFORMATION (PER SERVING):

Calories: 30

Fat: 2.5g

Carbs: 0.5g

Protein: 1.5g

CHIVE AND BACON OMELET

Here we have a simple keto version of the classic bacon and egg omelet. The addition of chive gives this dish a nice, mellow, onion hint; while the eggs, bacon and cheese keep this dish firmly in the keto diet's corner. Just a few minutes out of your busy morning and this tasty omelet is all yours!

SERVING SIZE:

This recipe yields 1 serving.

INGREDIENTS:

1 oz. cheddar cheese

1 tsp. bacon fat

2 slices bacon (cooked)

2 stalks cheddar

2 large eggs

Salt and pepper to taste

DIRECTIONS:

1. Make sure your chives are chopped, cheese shredded, eggs are cracked and mixed, and bacon cooked before you begin. Omelet making tends to be a fast process so keep on your toes and don't waste time completing these steps later!

2. Heat your bacon fat in a pan on medium-low heat.

3. Add your eggs, chives, and salt and pepper to the pan.

4. Cook until you can see the edges start to set, and then cook for another 30 seconds.

5. Immediately add your bacon to the center of the omelet, and turn off the heat.

6. Sprinkle your cheese on top of the bacon.

7. Fold two edges of the egg on top of the bacon/cheese pile. The melted cheese should hold the egg in place.

8. Repeat step 7 with the rest of the egg. This will create a slightly burrito shaped omelet.

9. Flip the omelet over, and allow it to cook a little longer in the pan (it'll still be warm).

10. Feel free to sprinkle some extra chive, cheese, or bacon on top.

There you go! A very fast paced recipe, but it'll leave you with a delicious start to the day.

NUTRITIONAL INFORMATION (PER SERVING):

Calories: 460

Fat: 36g

Carbs: 2g

Protein: 25g

BRIE AND RASPBERRY STUFFED WAFFLES

Start your day with panache and elegance as you whip up this unique creation. To call it a simple breakfast sandwich would be to offer insult, and here's why! This little gem takes almond flour and coconut milk to create keto friendly waffles; then fills them with a zesty combination of raspberry and brie to create a morning meal that will have you strutting out your door ready to take on the world.

SERVING SIZE:
This recipe yields 2 servings.

INGREDIENTS:
Waffles:

1 tsp. vanilla extract

1 tsp. baking powder

2 tbsp. flaxseed meal

1/2 cup almond flour

2 tbsp. swerve sweetener

7 drops liquid stevia

2 large eggs

1/3 cup coconut milk

Filling:

1 tbsp. lemon juice

1 tbsp. swerve sweetener

1/2 cup raspberries

zest of 1/2 lemon

2 tbsp. butter

3 oz. cream brie

DIRECTIONS:

1. Mix all the waffle ingredients in a container. Make sure your batter is smooth with no lumps.

2. Heat your waffle maker, and once it's hot, add your mixture.

3. Cook until either the indicator light says its ready or the steam dissipates.

4. Remove your waffles and repeat as necessary to cook all of your batter.

5. Slice your brie and drape over two of your four waffles. The waffles will still be warm and this will melt the brie.

6. In a pan, heat the swerve sweetener and butter

7. Just as the butter begins to bubble; add your raspberries, lemon juice, and zest.

8. Stir your raspberry mixture until it begins to bubble. As the mixture lets off steam, it will develop a jam-like consistency, and this is exactly what you want!

9. Now take the two waffle pieces with the brie, and broil them until the brie begins to bubble.

10. Pour/spread your raspberry jam on top of the brie waffles and cover with the other two waffles.

11. Grill the assembled waffle sandwich in the pan for a couple minutes until brown and crispy.

Enjoy!

NUTRITIONAL INFORMATION (PER SERVING):

Calories: 490

Fat: 40g

Carbs: 6g

Protein: 22g

BAKED AVOCADOS WITH EGGS AND BACON

We've all heard of stuffed peppers for dinner, but how about stuffed avocados for breakfast! Easy to make, and using just avocado, bacon, eggs, and pepper, these cups of early morning goodness are yours for the taking!

SERVING SIZE:

This recipe yields 1 serving.

INGREDIENTS:

2 small eggs

2 slices of bacon

1 avocado

Pepper to taste

DIRECTIONS:

1. Pan fry your bacon until it is just barely cooked

2. Preheat your oven to 425°F.

3. Halve the avocado and remove the seed.

4. Crumple some aluminum foil into ring shapes that will hold your avocado halves up on the baking sheet.

5. Break your eggs in a bowl, and spoon one yolk into each avocado half. Then continue to fill the hole of each avocado with egg whites until they're both full.

6. Crumble your bacon, and spread on top of the avocados.

Add pepper on top, and bake in the preheated oven for 12 to 15 minutes. After 10 minutes, check your eggs every minute or two to ensure you don't overcook them!

Serve them up!

NUTRITIONAL INFORMATION:

Calories: 700

Fat: 60g

Carbs: 6g

Protein: 23g

GREENIE PROTEIN SMOOTHIE

Sitting down to a pleasant, hot, morning breakfast is certainly a fantastic start to the day; but whether it is work, school, or simply being trapped under those comfortable blankets until the last moment, those rushed mornings always appear. However; you can be ready with this quick breakfast smoothie that saves on carbs while packing on the healthy fats to keep your diet running strong.

SERVING SIZE:

This recipe yields 1 serving.

INGREDIENTS:

1 scoop/0.9 oz. vanilla (or plain) whey protein powder (egg white powder)

2 tbsp. pistachio nuts

1 tsp. vanilla extract

6 drops liquid stevia

1/4 cup fresh spinach

1/4 cup coconut milk

1/4 cup fresh mint

1/2 avocado

1/2 cup water

Ice cubes (if desired)

DIRECTIONS:

1. Rinse your mint and spinach.

2. Peel and halve the avocado, and remove the seed.

3. Add all ingredients to a blender or food processor, and blend until smooth.

All done! Easy, right?

NUTRITIONAL INFORMATION (PER SERVING):

Calories: 490

Fat: 37g

Carbs: 9.5g

Protein: 26g

LAVENDER BISCUITS

Wake up feeling classy and ready for a suitably suave breakfast? Then look no further than these low carb lavender biscuits. Easy to make, packed with almond flour, and boasting a subtle lavender finish; these biscuits are perfect for a light and tasty breakfast. To take your game to the next level, check out our recipe for low carb peach jam as the perfect sidekick to these biscuits!

SERVING SIZE:

The recipe makes 6 servings.

INGREDIENTS:

4 eggs whites

1/3 cup coconut oil

1 1/2 cups almond flour

1 tbsp. lavender buds (culinary grade)

1 tsp. baking powder

4 drops liquid stevia

1 pinch kosher salt

DIRECTIONS:

1. Combine the coconut oil and almond flour in a bowl. Your hands would be the best tool for this job, and mix until there are pea-sized clumps of fat throughout the mixture.

2. Put the bowl of flour and oil in the refrigerator.

3. Whip your egg whites until they begin to foam, and add the salt, lavender, and baking powder. Mix well.

4. Add the egg mixture to the almond flour and oil, and mix well.

5. Use a tablespoon or ice cream scoop to place clumps of the mixture on a greased baking sheet.

6. Give each mound a slight pat so they're not round (think puffy pancake).

7. Bake at 350°F for 20 minutes or until golden brown.

Enjoy!

NUTRITIONAL INFORMATION (PER SERVING):

Calories: 270

Fat: 25g

Carbs: 4g

Protein: 10g

PEACHY CHIA JAM

Chia seeds have the very useful tendency to form a jelly-like consistency when mixed with liquid; which makes them the perfect choice for whipping up smoothies, jams, and puddings without using commercial gelatins. Here we'll call on these little fellows to help us put together a delicious jam consisting of peaches, chia seeds, low-carb sweetener, and lemon.

SERVING SIZE:

This recipe yields 10 servings.

INGREDIENTS:

2 tbsp. swerve sweetener

2 tbsp. chia seeds

1 tsp. lemon juice

2 cups peaches (chopped)

DIRECTIONS:

1. Combine your peaches, lemon juice, and sweetener in a blender; and blend until completely smooth.

2. Pour the smooth mixture into a bowl and add your chia seeds. Stir by hand until completely incorporated.

3. Pour your jam mixture into a jar or covered bowl, and place in the refrigerator. Let it cool and thicken for about an hour.

4. All done! Quick recipe and this jam will be the perfect accompaniment for many of your favorite breakfast pastries!

NUTRITIONAL INFORMATION (PER SERVING):

Calories: 30

Fat: 1g

Carbs: 3g

Protein: 1g

KETO STYLE MCMUFFIN

Who would have thought that you could enjoy a fast food breakfast sandwich while on the keto diet? But guess what? You can! The Keto Style McMuffin combines all the tastiness of its namesake, but slashes the carbs and ups the healthiness.

SERVING SIZE:

The recipe yields 2 servings.

INGREDIENTS:

Muffins:

1 large egg

2. tbsp. heavy whipping cream

1/4 tsp. baking soda

2 tbsp. water

1/4 cup cheddar cheese (grated)

1/4 cup flax meal

1/4 cup almond flour

1 pinch salt

Filling:

2 slices cheddar cheese

1 tbsp. butter

1 tbsp. ghee

2 large eggs

1 tsp. dijon mustard

4 slices crisp bacon

Salt and pepper to taste

DIRECTIONS:

1. Add all your dry ingredients for the muffins in a large bowl and mix well.

2. Drop in the eggs, cream, and water. Mix until completely smooth.

3. Add the grated cheese to the mixture and stir again. Don't worry if the cheese makes it clumpy, when you heat it everything will combine nicely.

4. Add your mixture to two single serving ramekins, and microwave on high for 60 to 90 seconds.

5. For the filling, cook your eggs on top of the ghee. Don't worry if they're not perfect circles. Do your best and you can trim later.

6. Now cut the cooked muffins in half, and spread your butter on each half.

7. Now stack 'em up! Layer your egg, mustard, bacon, and cheese for each muffin.

Enjoy! All the deliciousness of the classic McMuffin but completely guilt free!

NUTRITIONAL INFORMATION (PER SERVING):

Calories: 315

Fat: 55g

Carbs: 3g

Protein: 26g

Goat Cheese and Spinach Omelet

Omelets are the reliable go to breakfast for the keto diet. The eggs and cheese are bursting with healthy fats and protein, while you can still tailor each one to your tastes with an endless array of fillings. This goat cheese and spinach option is one such combination, we hope you enjoy!

Serving Size:

The recipe yields 1 serving.

Ingredients:

3 large eggs

1 medium spring onion

1 large handful of spinach

2 tbsp. heavy cream

2 tbsp. butter

1/4 onion

1 oz. goat cheese

Salt and pepper to taste

DIRECTIONS:

1. Heat a pan on medium, and add the butter. Spread the butter around the pan until it is completely melted.

2. Slice your onion (or dice it), and add to the pan once the butter begins to brown.

3. Caramelize your onion in the butter.

4. Once the onion is fully cooked and caramelized, add your spinach to the pan. Cook until the spinach is wilted.

5. Add salt and pepper to taste, give a final stir, and remove the spinach onion mix from the pan and set aside.

6. Now crack your eggs in a container (not the pan!); and add the cream and some salt and pepper. Mix everything together.

7. Now you can add your egg mixture to the pan, and cook until the edges jut begin to set.

8. Add your onion spinach mixture on **one** side of the egg, covering about half of the eggs.

9. Crumble your goat cheese over the onion and spinach.

10. Fold the other half of the egg over top of the onions, spinach, and cheese.

11. Remove from pan and garnish with more cheese if you like (who doesn't like more cheese?).

Serve it up and enjoy!

NUTRITIONAL INFORMATION (PER SERVING):

Calories: 615

Fat: 58g

Carbs: 5.4g

Protein: 26g

CREAMY COCONUT YOGURT

Wake up with a hankering for something savory, creamy, and delicious; but feel too guilty to have pudding for breakfast? Then grab this recipe for Creamy Coconut Yogurt! Coconut milk, cream and any toppings you like to give your day a scrumptious start!

This Recipe Yields about 2.5 cups of yogurt, and 1/2 cup equals one serving.

INGREDIENTS:

2/3 cup heavy whipping cream

2 capsules probiotic-10

1/2 tsp. xanthan gum

1 can coconut milk (full fat)

toppings (your choice!)

DIRECTIONS:

1. Pour the contents of your can of coconut milk into a container and stir well as the water and cream tend to separate (you can do this directly in the can too).

2. Put your coconut milk in a sealable container, and break the probiotic capsules into the milk, mix well, seal the container, and place in the oven (with the heat off and the oven light on). Let sit for 12 to 24 hours for the bacteria to culture.

3. After the sitting time, add your yogurt to a bowl and sprinkle in your xanthan gum. Mix completely.

4. In a separate bowl, use an electric mixer to whip your heavy cream until stiff peaks form.

5. Add the cream to the yogurt, and mix until you get the consistency you want. You can mix by hand or use an electric mixer if you wish.

6. Add whatever toppings you wish. Any kind of berry is sure to be delicious!

Enjoy your own, homemade, yogurt!

NUTRITIONAL INFORMATION (PER SERVING):

Calories: 310

Fat: 31g

Carbs: 4.5g

Protein: 0.5g

KETO PUMPKIN DONUT HOLES (WITH CARDAMOM)

Donut holes for breakfast? On the keto diet? Oh yes indeed, we've got you covered. These donut holes will keep you on your diet, and the addition of cardamom and pumpkin give these beauties a wonderfully unique taste.

SERVING SIZE:
The recipe yields 12 servings/donut holes.

INGREDIENTS:
1/4 tsp. vanilla extract

1/4 tsp. salt

1/4 tsp. orange extract

1 tsp. cardamom

3/4 tsp. liquid stevia

2 tbsp. erythritol

1 cup pumpkin puree (100%)

1/3 cup butter (melted)

1/2 cup coconut flour

3 large eggs

DIRECTIONS:

1. Melt your butter in the microwave. This generally takes about 20 to 30 seconds.

2. Add your eggs, vanilla extract, orange extract, and stevia to a large bowl. Mix well

3. In a separate bowl, combine your flour, erythritol, cardamom, and salt.

4. Now combine your egg mixture, pumpkin, and butter. Mix until smooth.

5. Sift, or slowly add, the dry ingredients into the wet, stirring continuously as you go.

6. You should have a sticky, dough like, mixture by now. Roll the dough into golf ball sized balls and place them in a cupcake tray.

7. Bake at 325°F for 18 to 25 minutes, or until they begin to brown.

8. Dust with cinnamon or any sweetener if you wish.

Wow your friends and enjoy!

NUTRITIONAL INFORMATION (PER SERVING):

Calories: 92

Fat: 7.5g

Carbs: 2.5g

Protein: 2g

KETO STYLE FRENCH TOAST MUFFINS

Everyone loves muffins. Everyone loves French toast too. So why not combine them? Or better yet, why not combine them AND keep them on the keto diet. Well friends, we've done just that.

SERVING SIZE:

The recipe yields 11 servings/muffins.

INGREDIENTS:

1 tsp. cinnamon

2 tbsp. erythritol

1 tsp. vanilla extract

1 tbsp. butter (unsalted)

2 tbsp. coconut oil

1/2 tsp. salt

1/4 tsp. nutmeg

1/4 cup heavy cream

1/4 cup peanut butter

1/4 cup toasted almonds (crushed)

6 large eggs

2/3 cup almond flour

10 drops liquid stevia

DIRECTIONS:

1. Preheat your oven to 350°F.

2. If your almonds aren't already toasted, grind them up in a food processor and add them to a pan heated to medium-high. Keep a close eye on them and stir occasionally.

3. Add your peanut butter, coconut oil, and butter to a bowl and microwave until completely melted (about 40 seconds). Mix completely.

4. Mix your erythritol, salt, cinnamon, almond flour, and nutmeg in a separate bowl.

5. Combine your melted butter mixture, the dry ingredients, and the heavy cream. Stir and mix completely.

6. Divide the mixture evenly in a cupcake tray and top with your toasted almonds.

7. Bake for approximately 20 to 25 minutes.

8. Give them about 5 minutes after removing from the oven to cool, and then remove from the cupcake tray. Allow them to cool for at least 15 minutes and top with whipped cream.

Serve them with a sprinkling of extra cinnamon or some berries if your wish!

NUTRITIONAL INFORMATION (PER SERVING):

Calories: 170

Fat: 16.5g

Carbs: 2.5g

Protein: 7g

FLAX SEED AND ALMOND PANCAKES

Ah yes, pancakes! Stacks and stacks of pancakes practically awash in syrup. You don't have to give up on these dreams with the keto diet. Our pancakes using almond flour and flax seeds keeps the carb count down will stacking the odds in favor of fats and protein.

SERVING SIZE:

The recipe yields 8 pancakes / servings.

INGREDIENTS:

4 large eggs

2 tbsp. erythritol

1 tsp. baking powder

1/2 tsp. nutmeg

2 tbsp. butter

1 tbsp. coconut flour

1/2 tsp. cinnamon

4 tbsp. coconut oil

1/2 cup almond flour

1/2 cup flax seed meal

1/2 cup coconut milk

Pinch of salt

DIRECTIONS:

1. In a bowl, mix all your dry ingredients.

2. Mix all your wet ingredients (except butter and coconut oil) in a separate bowl. Make sure ingredients are well combined and smooth.

3. Add the wet ingredients to the dry, stir constantly to get a smooth consistency.

4. Heat your pancake pan/griddle on medium-high, and grease with butter and coconut oil.

5. Add approximately 1/4 cup of your mixture to the pan.

6. Once bubbles form on top, allow to them to cook for another 30 seconds and then flip.

7. Repeat for the rest of your mixture.

8. Serve them up! Some sugar-free or homemade syrup would be the perfect accompaniment.

NUTRITIONAL INFORMATION (PER SERVING):

Calories: 215

Fat: 19g

Carbs: 2g

Protein: 6g

Waffle Disguised as Cinnamon Roll

Just as we offered you French toast combined with muffins, we offer a similarity sweet (in both senses of the word) combination to get your morning rolling, waffles and cinnamon rolls! Our low carb take on these two favorites will keep you on the keto diet while providing a mouth watering breakfast that your friends will covet.

SERVING SIZE:

The recipe yields 1 serving.

INGREDIENTS:

Waffle:

1/2 tsp. cinnamon

1/2 tsp. vanilla extract

1/4 tsp. baking soda

2 large eggs

1 tbsp. erythritol

6 tbsp. almond flour

Frosting:

1/4 tsp. vanilla extract

1 tbsp. erythritol

1/4 cinnamon

1 tbsp. heavy cream

2 tsp. batter from waffles

2 tbsp. cream cheese

DIRECTIONS:

1. For the waffles, mix all dry ingredients in a bowl.

2. In a separate bowl, mix all your wet ingredients together. Ensure that everything is mixed thoroughly.

3. Add the wet ingredients to the dry, mix until smooth.

4. Heat your waffle iron. When hot, add your batter and begin cooking. Remember to reserve 2 tsp. for the frosting

5. While the waffle is cooking, add your cream cheese and erythritol to a small bowl.

6. Now add the cinnamon, heavy cream, and batter. Mix completely so the mixture is smooth.

7. Once the waffle is finished cooking, remove from the iron, and spread your frosting over top.

Serve and enjoy!

NUTRITIONAL INFORMATION (PER SERVING):

Calories: 545

Fat: 52g

Carbs: 6g

Protein: 25g

DEVILED EGGS WITH BACON

Deviled eggs aren't just a fancy appetizer! Whip up these little devils with some bacon and a smidge of cayenne pepper to create a wonderfully satisfying and zippy breakfast for yourself.

SERVING SIZE:

The recipe yields 3 servings.

INGREDIENTS:

1 tsp. dijon mustard

1/2 tsp. rosemary

1 tbsp. bacon fat

1/4 tsp. cayenne pepper

2 slices bacon

1/4 cup mayonnaise (preferably homemade)

5 large eggs (hard boiled)

DIRECTIONS:

1. Slice/chop your bacon and toss them into a pan on medium heat. Remember they will shrink a little as they cook so don't chop too small!

2. Slowly cook the bacon until it is fully cooked and crispy.

3. Cut your hard boiled eggs in half, and scoop out the yolks.

4. Add the yolks, mayo, cayenne pepper, bacon fat, mustard, and **half** of your rosemary to a bowl and mix.

5. Add some of your crispy bacon to the holes left by the removed yolks, and fill the rest of the way with your yolk mixture.

Now garnish with the rest of your bacon and the remaining rosemary.

Enjoy!

NUTRITIONAL INFORMATION (PER SERVING):

Calories: 330

Fat: 29g

Carbs: 2g

Protein: 15g

Sausage Frittata

Big day ahead? Fill up with this keto friendly egg frittata stuffed with sausage to get your engine revved and ready for your day.

Serving Size:

The recipe yields 20 slices / servings.

Ingredients:

3/4 cup onion

2 cups cheddar cheese

1 medium green pepper

7 cups spinach

1/2 lb. Italian sausage

1/2 lb. chorizo

12 large eggs

8 tbsp. heavy cream

1 tbsp. olive oil

1 tsp. garlic powder

DIRECTIONS:

1. Heat your olive oil in a pan, and add the spinach.

2. Once the spinach wilts and cooks down, remove from the pan and start cooking the chorizo and sausage.

3. While this cooks, crack the eggs into a large bowl, add the heavy cream, and all spices. Mix completely.

4. Preheat your oven to 350°F.

5. When the sausage is cooked and crumbled, add it to the same reserve bowl as the spinach, but keep the sausage fat in the pan.

6. Now add your chopped onion and some pepper to the pan, and cooking until translucent. Add to bowl with spinach and sausage when done.

7. Now add your egg mixture to all your cooked ingredients and mix thoroughly.

8. Put the whole mixture in a foiled, and buttered, pan. Bake for approximately 45 minutes or when you can run a knife through the frittata and it comes up clean.

Slice it up and serve!

NUTRITIONAL INFORMATION (PER SERVING):

Calories: 175

Fat: 14g

Carbs: 1.2g

Protein: 12g

Scrambled Eggs with Spinach and Cheddar

Classic scrambled eggs are the perfect breakfast for the keto diet. Lots of fats and protein, and this recipe takes scrambled eggs to the next level by adding cheese and some spinach.

SERVING SIZE:

The recipe yields 1 serving.

INGREDIENTS:

1 tbsp. olive oil

1 tbsp. heavy cream

1 pinch each of salt and pepper

4 large eggs

4 cups spinach

1/2 cup cheddar cheese

DIRECTIONS:

1. Crack the eggs into a bowl, and add the heavy cream, salt, and pepper. Mix to your desired consistency.

2. Heat a large pan and throw in your olive oil.

3. When hot, add the spinach and as it begins to sizzle and wilt, add a little salt and pepper.

4. When the spinach is fully cooked and wilted, reduce heat to medium and add the egg mixture.

5. Stir slowly as the eggs begin to cook.

6. When the eggs have set, dump your cheese on top and allow to melt.

Enjoy!

NUTRITIONAL INFORMATION (PER SERVING):

Calories: 700

Fat: 55g

Carbs: 7g

Protein: 42g

Sausage and Feta Omelet

A filling omelet bursting with sausage and feta cheese is just the thing to start your day! Easy to make, this omelet will help keep your hunger, and diet, in check!

SERVING SIZE:

This recipe yields 1 serving.

INGREDIENTS:

1/2 tbsp. olive oil

1/4 cup half and half

1 tbsp. feta cheese

2 sausage links

3 large eggs

1 cup spinach

1 pinch black pepper and salt.

DIRECTIONS:

1. Heat two pans on medium, and add your oil to one of them

2. Mix your eggs with the half and half in a bowl, and add all your seasoning to this egg mixture.

3. Toss your sausage links into the pan that does not have the oil.

4. Add the spinach along with some salt and pepper to the pan with the oil.

5. Monitor the two pans, and when everything is cooked put it all in a single large bowl.

6. Add your egg mixture to the pan with the sausage fat.

7. When the edges of the eggs begin to set, add the sausage, spinach, and cheese.

8. Give it one more minute to cook, then flip half of the egg over to cover the insides.

9. Flip the whole omelet, and cook for a further 2 minutes. It helps if your cover the pan and allow the steam to cook the eggs as well.

Enjoy!

NUTRITIONAL INFORMATION (PER SERVING):

Calories: 540

Fat: 42g

Carbs: 2.5g

Protein: 30g

Classic Bacon and Eggs

No breakfast recipe list is complete without the classic bacon and eggs. Follow our simple recipe and enjoy this comforting breakfast.

SERVING SIZE:

This recipe yields 1 serving.

INGREDIENTS:

1 tbsp. butter

1 pinch each of salt and pepper

3 large eggs (room temperature)

4 slices bacon

1/3 cup heavy cream

DIRECTIONS:

1. Preheat your oven to 350°F.

2. Place the bacon on an oven sheet, and cook for 15 minutes until crispy.

3. Whisk your eggs and cream. Be gently as you whisk, we're not trying to beat the eggs.

4. Heat a pan on medium-low, and add the butter.

5. Once the butter has melted, add your egg mixture. Let sit until the eggs begin to set, then begin to stir.

6. Remove from the pan when the eggs are still ever so slightly runny, add your bacon, salt and pepper.

Enjoy!

NUTRITIONAL INFORMATION (PER SERVING):

Calories: 695

Fat: 65g

Carbs: 2.5g

Protein: 28g

KETO PUMPKIN PANCAKES

One of the staples of the autumn season is the sudden abundance of pumpkin recipes. Well let's not leave pumpkin pancakes out! This keto friendly recipe will let your whip up some truly delicious pancakes that are still great at any time of the year!

SERVING SIZE:

The recipe yields 8 servings.

INGREDIENTS:

1 tsp. pumpkin pie spice

2 tbsp. butter

1 tsp. baking powder

1/4 tsp. salt

1/4 cup pumpkin puree

1 cup almond meal

1/4 cup sour cream

2 large eggs

DIRECTIONS:

1. Combine your sour cream, butter, and eggs.

2. In a separate bowl, mix the baking powder, spice, salt, and almond meal.

3. Now slowly add the wet ingredients to the dry while stirring continuously. This will give you a nice smooth batter.

4. Heat a cast iron skillet on medium, and grease with butter.

5. Pour about 1/3 cup of your batter onto the skillet.

6. When bubbles begin to form on top, let cook for another minute, and then flip. Cook for one more minute.

7. Repeat steps 5 and 6 for the rest of your batter.

Serve 'em up with your favorite toppings!

NUTRITIONAL INFORMATION (PER SERVING):

Calories: 150

Fat: 11g

Carbs: 1.5g

Protein: 5.5g

KETO QUICHE

Have guests for breakfast? Then impress them with this delicious, keto friendly, quiche recipe. Or whip it up on a weekend and keep it all to yourself!

SERVING SIZE:
This recipe yields 8 slices/servings.

INGREDIENTS:
Crust:

1/4 cup olive oil

1/4 tsp. salt

1 tsp. oregano (dried)

1 1/2 almond four

Filling:

1/2 tsp. pepper

1/4 tsp. salt

1 tsp. garlic

1 tsp. Mrs. Dash (table blend)

1 1/2 cups cheddar cheese

1 green bell pepper

6 large eggs

6 slices of bacon

DIRECTIONS:

1. Preheat your oven to 350°F.

2. Slice your bacon into good sized chunks, and add them to a stovetop pan heated on medium.

3. Add ALL of the crust ingredients to a bowl and use your hands to mix. When fully mixed, form a ball and press the dough into an 11x7 casserole dish.

4. Bake the crust for about 20 minutes and remove. It won't be cooked all the way! It will continue to cook as the fillings bake.

5. When the bacon finishes cooking, remove and add the green peppers and garlic to the pan. Cook in the bacon fat while keeping the pan on medium heat.

6. In a separate bowl, combine all the seasoning, cheese, eggs, bacon, pepper, and garlic. You can toss in the fat from the pan if you wish.

7. Pour the mixture into the crust and bake for 16 to 18 minutes.

Allow to cook and enjoy!

NUTRITIONAL INFORMATION (PER SERVING):

Calories: 330

Fat: 30g

Carbs: 3.8g

Protein: 11.5g

Keto Chicken Frittata

Feeling eggy this morning? Then this chicken frittata is for you! Healthy chicken baked into an egg pie; this keto recipe is overflowing with healthy fats and protein.

Serving Size:

The recipe yields 8 slices/servings.

Ingredients:

1 1/2 cup cheddar cheese

10 large eggs

2 1/2 Bella mushrooms (chopped)

3 cups spinach (chopped)

3 chicken sausages

2 tsp. hot sauce (your choice)

1 tbsp. ranch dressing

1/2 tsp. Mrs. Dash (table blend)

DIRECTIONS:

1. Preheat oven to 400°F.

2. Chop your sausages, and start cooking in a cast iron skillet on medium high. We're aiming for nice and crisp sausages here.

3. When the sausages are approaching fully cooked, toss in the spinach and mushrooms.

4. In a separate container, crack the eggs and mix with your ranch, hot sauce, and spaces. Mix everything completely.

5. Once the spinach and mushrooms are cooked, pour in your eggs as well as the cheese. Give this several stirs to make sure everything is combined in the pan.

6. Now slide your pan into the oven for 10 minutes.

7. Finish it up with a 3 to 4 minute broil.

Slice it up and serve!

NUTRITIONAL INFORMATION (PER SLICE):

Calories: 235

Fat: 18g

Carbs: 3g

Protein: 20g

KETO BREAKFAST LAYER

Feeling utterly ravenous? This cook up this breakfast made of layers of bacon, egg, and cheese! Perfect for getting your cheese and bacon craving under control.

SERVING SIZE:

This recipe yields 4 servings.

INGREDIENTS:

1/4 tsp. salt

1/4 tsp black pepper

2 tbsp. heavy cream

1/4 tsp. Mrs. Dash (table blend)

4 cups spinach

4 large eggs

10 slices bacon

2 tbsp. bacon grease

1/2 cup cheddar cheese

DIRECTIONS:

1. Preheat oven to 400°F.

2. Weave your bacon into about a 5x5 slap. Think of how a basket weave works, but with bacon!

3. Bake the bacon weave for about 25 minutes, until fully cooked. Remove and place on paper towel.

4. Add your bacon grease to a stovetop pan, and toss in the spinach.

5. When the spinach is cooked and wilted, add the eggs and all the seasoning.

6. Slowly scramble the eggs until fully cooked.

7. Spread the cooked eggs on top of the bacon weave.

8. Top the eggs with the cheese and broil for 4 minutes.

9. There you go! Let it cool and then cut into 4 pieces.

NUTRITIONAL INFORMATION (PER SERVING):

Calories: 305

Fat: 26g

Carbs: 2g

Protein: 18g

KETO COFFEE CAKE

Coffee cake isn't just for the carb carefree anymore! Follow this recipe in using almond flour for your cake and you'll get to enjoy this delectable breakfast indulgence too!

SERVING SIZE:

This recipe yields 8 slices/servings.

INGREDIENTS:

Base:

1/4 tsp. liquid stevia

1/4 tsp. cream of tartar

2 tsp. vanilla extract

1/4 cup protein powder (unflavored)

6 oz. cream cheese

1/4 cup erythritol

6 eggs (separated)

Filling:

1/2 stick butter

1/4 cup erythritol

1 tbsp. cinnamon

1 1/2 cup almond flour

1/4 cup maple syrup substitute

DIRECTIONS:

1. Preheat oven to 325°F.

2. Add your egg yolks and erythritol to a bowl, and cream.

3. Add all remaining ingredients for the base (except cream of tartar and egg whites), and whisk together.

4. Separately, whip the egg whites and cream of tartar together until stiff peaks form.

5. Slowly fold 1/2 of the egg white mixture into the egg yolks mixture. Be gentle as you complete this process! Now add the remaining 1/2.

6. Now, in a separate container, mix all of the ingredients for the filling. Mix until a dough forms.

7. Pour your base mixture into a metal cake pan. Top with half of the filling. You may have to push this down a little if it doesn't sink through on its own.

8. Bake for 20 minutes, and then add the rest of the filling to the top.

9. Bake a further 25 to 30 minutes. A toothpick inserted in the middle should come up clean.

10. Let cool for 20 minutes and then remove.

Enjoy!

NUTRITIONAL INFORMATION (PER SLICE):

Calories: 255

Fat: 25g

Carbs: 3.2g

Protein: 13g

KETO CHIVE SOUFFLÉ

This delicious soufflé combing cheese, ham, and eggs will definitely start your day on the right path. Stuffed full of good fats as well to keep you on the keto diet!

SERVING SIZE:

The recipe yields 5 servings.

INGREDIENTS:

1 tbsp. butter

3 tbsp. fresh chives (chopped)

6 large eggs

6 oz. ham steak (cooked and cubed)

1 1/2 garlic (minced)

1/2 onion (diced)

3 tbsp. olive oil

1 cup cheddar cheese

1/2 cup heavy cream

1/2 tsp. salt

1/4 tsp. black pepper

DIRECTIONS:

1. Preheat oven to 400°F.

2. Heat olive oil in a stovetop pan. Once hot, add your onions.

3. When the onions become translucent, add the garlic. Continue to cook until they begin to brown.

4. In a separate bowl, mix the rest of the ingredients. Once combined, add the onion and garlic to the mix.

5. Divide the mixture evenly between 5 ramekins.

6. Bake for approximately 20 minutes.

Allow to cool and enjoy!

NUTRITIONAL INFORMATION (PER SERVING):

Calories: 400

Fat: 41g

Carbs: 3g

Protein: 20g

Breakfast Burger with Peanut Butter

Burger for breakfast? We've got you covered. But we're changing things up with the addition of peanut butter!

Serving Size:

This recipe yields 2 servings.

Ingredients:

2 large eggs

1 tbsp. butter

4 slices bacon

1 tbsp. PB fit powder

2 oz. pepper jack cheese

4 oz. sausage

Salt and pepper to taste

DIRECTIONS:

1. Preheat oven to 400°F.

2. Bake your bacon in the oven for 25 minutes, or until fully cooked.

3. Mix the butter and PB fit powder together. Set this aside for later use.

4. Use your hands to form the sausage into the traditional burger patty shape. There should be 2.

5. Cook these patties on a stovetop pan over medium heat. Once cooked, add the cheese and cover with a pan to allow it to melt.

6. Now separately cook your eggs over easy.

7. Assemble! Arrange the burger, eggs, and bacon to make your breakfast burger stack, and top with the PB butter mixture.

Enjoy!

NUTRITIONAL INFORMATION (PER SERVING):

Calories: 650

Fat: 55g

Carbs: 3.5g

Protein: 29g

"You don't need a silver fork to eat good food."

-Paul Prudhomme

KETOGENIC DIET

30 LUSCIOUS LUNCHES

1 MONTH OF LOW-CARB, HIGH-FAT WEIGHT LOSS MEALS

Recipes365

SOUTHERN PORK STEW

Those midday slumps can certainly put the rest of your day on a slippery slide. We're tired, we're getting hungry, and during the winter months the feeling to crawl under a blanket for a nap can be almost overwhelming. But fear not! We have the perfect dish that will put some warmth in your belly and a spring in your step. Ready? Well here we go.

SERVING SIZE:

You'll get 4 servings.

INGREDIENTS:

Spices:

1 tsp. oregano

1 tsp. paprika

¼ tsp. cinnamon

1 tsp. minced garlic

2 tsp. cumin

2. tsp. chilli powder

2 bay leaves

Salt and pepper to taste (approx ½ tsp. each)

Meat:

1 lb. cooked pork shoulder (sliced)

Vegetables:

½ green bell pepper (sliced)

½ red bell pepper (Sliced)

½ medium onion

6 oz. button mushrooms

½ jalapeno (sliced)

Soup:

¼ cup tomato paste

2 cups chicken broth

2 cups gelatinous bone broth

Juice: ½ lime

½ cup coffee (your remedy for the midday slump)

DIRECTIONS:

1. Clean and slice all your vegetables.

2. Add two tablespoons of Olive Oil to a pan and turn to high heat.

3. Sauté your vegetables until they are just beginning to cook and filling your kitchen with their fantastic aroma. Be careful not to overcook them here! That will give you a slightly mushy stew later on.

4. Set your slow cooker on low; add the bone broth, coffee, and chicken broth.

5. While your slow cooker is warming, add spices and bay leaves to a single bowl. This is a handy step for almost any recipe and will help you keep all your spices in one place.

6. Now add all your mushrooms and sliced pork to the slow cooker.

7. Give your cooking vegetables and oil a final stir, and add them to the crock pot along with all your spices.

8. Cover, and let the slow cooker work its magic for about 4-10 hours.

9. Once it's finished, remove the bay leaves (or keep an eye out for them), and serve!

And there you have it; a simple, hearty and unique dish to add a little sunshine to your lunchtime. Enjoy!

NUTRITIONAL INFORMATION (PER SERVING):

Calories: 386

Fat: 29g

Carbs: 6.5g

Protein: 19.8g

KETO BACON CHICKEN SANDWICH WITH AVOCADO

Sandwiches are no longer off limits on the keto diet! Make your bread using egg and cream cheese to keep the fat and protein content up, and top it with cheese and avocado!

SERVING SIZE:

The recipe yields 2 servings.

INGREDIENTS:

Bread:

1/4 tsp. salt

1/2 tsp. garlic powder

1/8 tsp. cream of tartar

3 large eggs

3 oz. cream cheese

Filling:

3 oz. chicken

2 slices bacon

2 slices pepper jack cheese

1 tsp. sriracha

1 tbsp. mayonnaise

2 grape tomatoes

1/4 avocado

DIRECTIONS:

1. Preheat oven to 300°F.

2. Separate your eggs into different bowls.

3. Add cream of tartar and salt to the eggs whites, and whip until you get soft peaks.

4. Add cream cheese to the egg yolks bowl and beat until a uniform pale yellow color forms.

5. Fold the egg white mixture into the yolks. Gently complete this as we want to the whites nice and airy.

6. Line a baking sheet with parchment paper, and pour about 1/4 cup of your bread mixture into individual areas, and form into square shapes.

7. Sprinkle garlic atop the bread and bake for 25 minutes.

8. While the bread is baking, cook the chicken and bacon with a little salt and pepper.

9. Once everything is cooked, assemble your sandwich with the mayo, avocado, cheese, and tomatoes.

Enjoy!

NUTRITIONAL INFORMATION (PER SERVING):

Calories: 355

Fat: 28g

Carbs: 1.5g

Protein: 24g

Spring Salad

Enjoy this light and sweet salad to keep you going for the afternoon. Bacon and pine nuts will help fill you up while the raspberry vinaigrette gives a distinctly sweet flavor.

SERVING SIZE:

This recipe yields 1 serving.

INGREDIENTS:

2 tbsp. parmesan (shaved)

2 tbsp. raspberry vinaigrette

2 oz. mixed greens

3 tbsp. pine nuts (roasted)

2 slices bacon

Salt and pepper to taste

DIRECTIONS:

1. Cook the bacon in a stovetop pan. Nice and crispy is what we're aiming for here!

2. Assemble your salad with the rest of the ingredients and crumble the bacon overtop.

3. Shake well to make sure everything in combined

Enjoy!

NUTRITIONAL INFORMATION (PER SERVING):

Calories: 470

Fat: 36g

Carbs: 4g

Protein: 17.5g

CHICKEN EGG SOUP

Easy and delicious lunchtime soup! Chicken broth and eggs yield a very savory dish while the extremely easy preparation makes it the perfect choice for a quick lunch.

SERVING SIZE:

This recipe yields 1 serving.

INGREDIENTS:

2 large eggs

1 tbsp. bacon fat

1 tsp. chili garlic paste

1/2 cube chicken bouillon

1 1/2 cups chicken broth

DIRECTIONS:

1. Heat a pan on medium-high, and add the broth, bacon fat, and bouillon cube.

2. Once the soup begins to boil, add the chili paste and stir continually for a minute. Now remove from heat.

3. Beat the eggs in a separate container, and pour into the broth.

4. Stir and let sit for about 30 seconds.

Serve and enjoy!

NUTRITIONAL INFORMATION (PER SERVING):

Calories: 275

Fat: 24g

Carbs: 2g

Protein: 13g

JALAPENO MUG CAKE

Missing out on lunch is a recipe for a disastrous afternoon. But even on the tightest of schedules, a quick mug cake can still get you a filling lunch! Here we have a zesty jalapeno mug cake made of egg and almond flour.

SERVING SIZE:
This recipe yields 1 serving.

INGREDIENTS:
1 large egg

1 tbsp. cream cheese

1 tbsp. butter

1 slice bacon

1/2 tsp. baking powder

1/2 jalapeno pepper

2 tbsp. almond flour

1 tbsp. golden flaxseed meal

1/4 tsp. salt

DIRECTIONS:

1. Heat a pan over medium, and cook the bacon until nice and crisp.

2. Now in a mug, mix all of the remaining ingredients. Scrape down the sides so everything is in the bottom of the mug.

3. Microwave for 80 seconds on high.

4. Flip the mug upside down and gently tap against a plate to make the cake fall out, and garnish with the bacon and any leftover jalapenos.

Enjoy!

NUTRITIONAL INFORMATION (PER SERVING):

Calories: 430

Fat: 36g

Carbs: 5g

Protein: 16g

ENCHILADA SOUP

This rich soup will certainly spice up your lunchtime! Chicken, cheese, and a little cayenne pepper will keep you running and on the keto diet at the same time.

SERVING SIZE:
The recipe yields 4 servings.

INGREDIENTS:
8 oz. cream cheese

4 cups chicken broth

6 oz. chicken (shredded)

4 stalks celery (diced)

1 red bell pepper (diced)

3 tbsp. olive oil

1/2 tsp. cayenne pepper

1/2 lime (juiced)

2 tsp. cumin

1 tsp. chili powder

1 tsp. oregano

2 tsp. garlic

1 cup tomatoes (diced)

1/2 cup cilantro (chopped)

DIRECTIONS:

1. Heat the olive oil in a pan on medium. Once hot, add the celery and pepper.

2. Once the celery is soft, toss in your tomatoes and cook until they begin to release their juice.

3. Add all your spices to the pan, and stir several times to incorporate.

4. Now add your cilantro and chicken broth to the pot, and crank up the heat to bring to a boil.

5. Once boiling, reduce heat to low, and simmer for 25 minutes.

6. Now add your cream cheese and again bring to a boil, then reduce heat, then simmer again for 30 minutes.

7. Add the shredded chicken to the pot as well as the lime juice. Stir several times to make sure everything is well mixed.

All set! Feel free to garnish with some cilantro or more cheese!

NUTRITIONAL INFORMATION (PER SERVING):

Calories: 350

Fat: 30g

Carbs: 5g

Protein: 14g

KETO PEPPER AND BASIL PIZZA

Lose the carb filled flour behind and swap in almond meal for the crust to this delicious lunchtime pizza. Keep it light with peppers and basil or pile on the meat, either way this is a keto friendly dish!

SERVING SIZE:
This recipe yields 2 servings (1/2 of one pizza).

INGREDIENTS:
Crust:

1 large egg

2 tbsp. cream cheese

2 tbsp. psyllium husk

1 tsp. Italian seasoning

2 tbsp. parmesan cheese

6 oz. mozzarella cheese

1/2 cup almond flour

1/2 tsp. each of salt and pepper

Toppings:

1/4 cup tomato sauce

3 tbsp. fresh basil (chopped)

4 oz. cheddar cheese (shredded)

2/3 bell pepper

1 vine tomato

DIRECTIONS:

1. Preheat your oven to 400°F.

2. Give your mozzarella (for the crust) a quick 45 second zap in the microwave to melt it.

3. Add all the other crust ingredients to the cheese and mix together completely.

4. Use your hands, or a rolling pin, to flatten the dough and make a circle.

5. Bake this for 10 minutes, and remove from the oven.

6. Now throw on all your toppings, and bake for an additional 10 minutes.

7. Remove pizza and let it cool

It's all yours!

NUTRITIONAL INFORMATION (PER SERVING):

Calories: 420

Fat: 30g

Carbs: 6g

Protein: 25g

Breezy Caprese Salad

Piles and piles of tomatoes, mozzarella and basil, what could be better? This simple lunch is delicious and filling, especially for those cheese hounds out there.

SERVING SIZE:

The recipe yields 2 servings.

INGREDIENTS:

3 tbsp. olive oil

6 oz. mozzarella cheese

1 tomato

1/4 cup fresh basil (chopped)

Black pepper and salt to taste

DIRECTIONS:

1. Use a blender, or food processor, to pulse the basil and olive oil. This will leave you will a basil paste.

2. Now slice your tomato into about 1/4 "slices. We're looking for 6 slices here, so feel free to grab another tomato if you need to!

3. Cut the mozzarella into 1 oz. slices (right about the same size as the tomatoes or slightly thicker).

4. Layer your Caprese with the tomato as the base, then cheese, and topped with basil paste.

5. Season with salt and pepper to taste.

Dig in! Feel free to garnish with extra olive oil.

NUTRITIONAL INFORMATION (PER SERVING):

Calories: 406

Fat: 35g

Carbs: 5g

Protein: 17g

KETO PEANUT SHRIMP CURRY

No need to stick to the hurried, unsatisfying, lunches we're used to. Give things a unique twist with this dish featuring shrimp and curry!

SERVING SIZE:

This recipe yields 2 servings.

INGREDIENTS:

1 tsp. fish sauce

1 tbsp. peanut butter

1 tsp. ginger (minced)

1 tsp. roasted garlic (crushed)

1 tbsp. soy sauce

1/4 tsp. xanthan gum

1/2 tsp. turmeric

3 tbsp. cilantro (chopped)

2 tbsp. coconut oil

1 spring onion (chopped)

1 cup vegetable stock

1/2 cup sour cream

1 cup coconut milk

5 oz. broccoli florets

2 tbsp. green curry paste

6 oz. shrimp (cooked)

1/2 lime (juiced)

DIRECTIONS:

1. Heat a pan over medium, and add the coconut oil. When hot, toss in the garlic, spring onion, and ginger.

2. Stir for a few minutes; and once cooked, add 1 tbsp. of the green curry paste. Along with your soy sauce, turmeric, peanut butter and fish sauce.

3. Continue to stir and cook for several minutes.

4. Now add the vegetable broth and coconut milk.

5. Add the xanthan gum, and mix completely.

6. When you notice the mixture begin to thicken, toss in the broccoli.

7. Continue to stir, and add the cilantro.

8. Lastly; add the shrimp and mix everything up. Allow it to cook for a few more minutes to allow the shrimp taste to develop.

Serve with your sour cream on top and enjoy!

NUTRITIONAL INFORMATION (PER SERVING):

Calories: 450

Fat: 32g

Carbs: 8.5g

Protein: 28g

CUCUMBER SALAD

Just like a mug cake, a salad can be the quick and easy solution to a hectic midday. Throw this cucumber salad together in mere minutes and enjoy the combination of noodles and cucumber.

SERVING SIZE:

This recipe yields 1 serving.

INGREDIENTS:

1/4 tsp. red pepper flakes

1 tbsp. rice vinegar

1 tbsp. sesame oil

1 tsp. sesame seeds

2 tbsp. olive oil

1 spring onion

1 packet shirataki noodles

3/4 large cucumber

salt and pepper to taste

DIRECTIONS:

1. Thoroughly rinse and wash your shirataki noodles, and allow them to dry on a paper towel.

2. Heat a pan over medium-high, and add the coconut oil.

3. Once the pan is hot, add your noodles and fry them for 6 minutes. They should shrink a great deal and any extra liquid will boil off.

4. Remove the noodles from the pan and again set them on a paper towel to dry.

5. Slice the cucumber into whatever sized slices you want, and arrange over a plate. Now top the cucumber with all the other ingredients (other than the noodles), and set in the fridge for 30 minutes.

6. Remove from the fridge, top with the noodles, and serve.

Enjoy!

NUTRITIONAL INFORMATION (PER SERVING):

Calories: 415

Fat: 44g

Carbs: 6g

Protein: 2g

PIZZAS ON PORTOBELLO

Don't want the carbs of ordinary pizza crust, but don't have the time to make your own? Then just throw down a couple Portobello mushrooms! These mushroom caps provide the perfect base to your midday pizza, and you can cook them to crispy or keep them soft, whichever you prefer!

SERVING SIZE:

This recipe yields 4 servings.

INGREDIENTS:

4 oz. mozzarella cheese

20 slices pepperoni

4 large Portobello mushroom caps

1 medium tomato

6 tbsp. olive oil

1/4 cup fresh basil (chopped)

salt and pepper to taste

DIRECTIONS:

1. Scrape the insides out from the mushroom caps. You want to just a have a shell here.

2. Coat the tops (not the insides) of the caps with your olive oil, and season with salt and pepper.

3. Broil the mushrooms for about 4 minutes, then flip and broil for an additional 3 to 4 minutes.

4. Slice your tomato into thin pieces, and place in the scooped out portion of the mushrooms.

5. Top the tomato with the basil

6. Now top the basil with the pepperoni slices and mozzarella cubes.

7. Broil for 3 to 4 minutes or until cheese starts to bubble.

All set to enjoy!

NUTRITIONAL INFORMATION (PER SERVING):

Calories: 320

Fat: 33g

Carbs: 2.5g

Protein: 8g

GINGER GLAZED SALMON

This savory ginger covered salmon is sure to put a smile on your face. A quick recipe with a savory combination of spices, this is sure to become a lunchtime favorite.

SERVING SIZE:

This recipe yields 2 servings.

INGREDIENTS:

1 tbsp. red boat fish sauce

2 tsp. garlic (minced)

1 tbsp. ketchup (sugar free)

1 tsp. ginger (minced)

1 tbsp. rice vinegar

2 tbsp. white wine

2 tbsp. soy sauce

2 tsp. sesame oil

10 oz. salmon fillet

DIRECTIONS:

1. Toss all of your ingredients except for the ketchup, white wine, and sesame oil into a container. Let these marinate for about 15 minutes.

2. Heat a pan on high and add the sesame oil.

3. As soon as the oil lets off a little smoke, add the fish with the skin side down.

4. Allow the fish skin to crisp up and cook, then flip and continue cooking. It generally takes about 3 to 4 minutes per side. After the first flip, add all the marinade ingredients to the pan and let them cook with the fish.

5. When cooked, remove the salmon from the pan. Add the ketchup and white wine to the liquid left in the pan.

6. Let everything simmer for 6 minutes, and put in side dish.

Serve it up with the sauce on the side.

NUTRITIONAL INFORMATION (PER SERVING):

Calories: 375

Fat: 22g

Carbs: 2g

Protein: 34g

EGG STUFFED AVOCADO

Turn the tables on the deviled egg! Instead of stuffing an egg, it's time to stuff an avocado with egg salad. Full of healthy fats and delicious spices, this easy recipe is a joy to prepare and eat.

SERVING SIZE:

This recipe yields 6 servings (each half of avocado is one serving).

INGREDIENTS:

2 tsp. brown mustard

1 tsp. hot sauce

4 tbsp. mayonnaise

2 tbsp. fresh lime juice

1/2 tsp. cumin

1/3 red onion

6 large eggs (hard boiled)

3 stalks celery

3 avocados

Salt and pepper to taste

DIRECTIONS:

1. Chop your onion, celery, and hard-boiled eggs.

2. In a bowl, combine all of the ingredients except the avocado.

3. Slice each avocado in half lengthwise and remove the pit.

4. Spoon your egg salad mixture into the center of each avocado slice.

Enjoy!

NUTRITIONAL INFORMATION (PER SERVING):

Calories: 300

Fat: 27g

Carbs: 4g

Protein: 8g

KETO TOMATO PESTO MUG CAKE

Another mug cake recipe for those hectic lunches! This tomato and pesto filled cake is tasty, and would make an excellent addition to some Caprese salad!

SERVING SIZE:

The recipe yields 1 serving.

INGREDIENTS:

2 tbsp. butter

2 tbsp. almond flour

1 large egg

1/2 tsp. baking powder

Pesto:

1 tbsp. almond flour

5 tsp. sun dried tomato pesto

1 pinch salt

DIRECTIONS:

1. Combine all ingredients in a mug (keep some pesto in reserve if you want it as a topping).

2. Microwave the mug on high for 70 to 80 seconds.

3. Light tap the mug against a plate and the mug will fall out.

4. Top with any leftover pesto

Quick and easy, enjoy!

NUTRITIONAL INFORMATION (PER SERVING):

Calories: 460

Fat: 45g

Carbs: 4g

Protein: 13g

KETO CABBAGE ROLLS WITH CORNED BEEF

These corned beef cabbage rolls are delicious, filling, and make a wonderful presentation if you're entertaining. The subtle hint of cloves and allspice provide an excellent finish to this dish!

SERVING SIZE:
This recipe yields 5 servings:

INGREDIENTS:
1 tbsp. erythritol

1 tbsp. bacon fat

1 fresh lemon

1 tbsp. brown mustard

1 tsp. whole peppercorns

2 tsp. Worcestershire sauce

1 tsp. mustard seeds

1/4 tsp. cloves

1/4 allspice

1/2 tsp. red pepper flakes

2 tsp. salt

1/4 cup coffee

1 medium onion

1/4 cup white wine

15 large cabbage leaves

1.5 lbs. corned beef

1 bay leaf (crushed)

DIRECTIONS:

1. In a slow cooker, combine all your spices, liquids, and the corned beef.

2. Turn the slow cooker to low, and leave for 6 hours.

3. When ready, bring a pot of water to boiling, and add all cabbage leaves as well as the sliced onion.

4. After 3 minutes remove the cabbage leaves, and dump them in some ice water for a further 4 minutes. Remember the onions should still be in the boiling water!

5. Slice the meat and dry off the cabbage leaves. Remove the onion from the water.

6. All the fillings into each cabbage leaf, and give a squirt of lemon juice overtop for good measure.

Enjoy!

NUTRITIONAL INFORMATION (PER SERVING):

Calories: 475

Fat: 27g

Carbs: 4g

Protein: 34.5g

KETO SAUSAGE PEPPER SOUP

This hearty soup is perfect for a drizzly lunchtime. It will leave your house, or office, with a wonderful aroma and the addition of hot sausage and jalapenos are sure to give you a kick!

SERVING SIZE:
This recipe yields 4 servings.

INGREDIENTS:
2 tsp. chili powder

2 tsp. garlic (minced)

2 tsp. cumin

1 tsp. Italian seasoning

1 green bell pepper

6 cups raw spinach

1/2 medium onion

1 can tomatoes with jalapenos

1.4 lbs. hot Italian sausage

2 cups beef stock

1/2 tsp. salt

1 red bell pepper

DIRECTIONS:

1. Tear the sausage into chunks and cook on the stove until fully cooked.

2. Slice your peppers; and add them, tomatoes, all spices, and beef stock to a crock pot.

3. Top the crock pot with the sausage and mix.

4. Fry your onions and garlic until the garlic begins to brown.

5. Add the onions and garlic to the crock pot, and top with the spinach.

6. Turn the crock pot to high, and cook for 3 hours.

7. After 3 hours, open it up and give everything a stir, then cook a further 2 hours.

Serve it up!

NUTRITIONAL INFORMATION (PER SERVING):

Calories: 380

Fat: 28g

Carbs: 7g

Protein: 25g

Coconut Curry

Would all the coconut lovers please stand up. We hope that includes most of you because this fantastic combination of curry and coconut is certain to give your lunch hour a zing!

SERVING SIZE:

This recipe yields 2 servings.

INGREDIENTS:

2 tsp. red boat fish sauce

1 tsp. garlic (minced)

2 tsp. soy sauce

1 tsp. ginger (minced)

1/2 cup coconut cream (or coconut milk)

4 tbsp. coconut oil

1 cup broccoli florets

1 tbsp. red curry paste

1/4 onion

1 large handful spinach

DIRECTIONS:

1. Add 2 tbsp. coconut oil to a pan on medium-high.

2. Chop your onion, and add it as well as the garlic to the pan.

3. When the garlic begins to brown, turn heat down to medium, and add broccoli.

4. Stir everything together, and when the broccoli is partially cooked, move everything to one side of the pan.

5. Add the curry paste to the open side of the pan, and let cook for 60 seconds.

6. Now toss the spinach on top of the broccoli until it begins to wilt, then add the coconut cream and rest of the oil.

7. Stir everything together, and add the fish sauce, ginger, and soy sauce. Let simmer for 10 minutes.

Enjoy!

NUTRITION INFORMATION (PER SERVING):

Calories: 395

Fat: 40g

Carbs: 7g

Protein: 6g

KETO TURKEY MEATBALLS

If it's a 'plate of meatballs all to myself' kind of day, or if you're in charge of appetizers for a party, these keto friendly turkey meatballs are just the ticket!

SERVING SIZE:

This recipe yields 20 servings/meatballs.

INGREDIENTS:

1/2 salt

1/2 pepper

3 sprigs thyme

2 large handfuls of spinach

3 small red chilies

10 slices bacon

2 lbs. ground turkey

1/2 green pepper

2 large eggs

1 oz. pork rinds

1 small onion

DIRECTIONS:

1. Line a baking sheet with foil, and place bacon on top. Preheat oven to 400°F.

2. Bake the bacon for 30 minutes, or until desired crispiness is reached.

3. While the bacon is cooking, add all ingredients (except ground turkey and spinach) to a food processor and mince well.

4. Add the minced mixture to the ground turkey and mix well.

5. Once the bacon is done, drain the fat into an individual container.

6. Now form 20 meatballs from your mixture and place on the same baking sheet that you used before.

7. Cook meatballs for 20 minutes or until the juice begins to run clear.

8. Skewer 2 to 3 pieces of bacon to each meatball.

9. Now in a food processor, blend the spinach, leftover bacon fat, and any spices you wish until you have a paste.

Serve the meatballs on top of the paste and enjoy!

NUTRITIONAL INFORMATION (PER SERVING):

Calories: 140

Fat: 10.5g

Carbs. 0.5g

Protein: 11g

Pumpkin Soup

A mellow soup bursting with autumn spice and pumpkin, this soup is perfect for fending off the cold as the seasons change. It's also an excellent remedy for a rainy day!

Serving Size:

This recipe yields 3 servings (1 cup each).

Ingredients:

1/2 tsp. pepper

1/2 tsp. salt

1/4 tsp. ginger (minced)

1/4 tsp. coriander

1/8 tsp. nutmeg

1/4 tsp. cinnamon

2 cloves garlic (roasted and minced)

4 tbsp. butter

1 cup pumpkin puree

1/2 cup heavy cream

4 slices bacon

1 bay leaf

1/4 onion (chopped)

3 tbsp. bacon grease

1 1/2 cups chicken broth

DIRECTIONS:

1. Add the butter to a sauce pan over medium-low heat, and heat until it begins to brown.

2. When the butter is dark golden in color, add your garlic, ginger, and onions

3. Cook for 3 minutes, and once the onions are translucent, add all of your spices and stir completely.

4. Cook for a further 2 minutes; then add the chicken broth and pumpkin.

5. Increase heat and bring to a boil. Once boiling, reduce heat and simmer for 20 minutes.

6. Transfer everything to a blender and puree until smooth or desired consistency.

7. Return to pot and simmer for a further 20 minutes.

8. Now cook your bacon in whatever style you wish.

9. When the soup is ready, add heavy cream and bacon grease. Mix well.

10. Crumble your bacon on top and serve.

Savor and enjoy!

NUTRITIONAL INFORMATION (PER SERVING):

Calories: 485

Fat: 47g

Carbs: 7.5g

Protein: 6g

CHICKEN SATAY

The upbeat combination of cayenne pepper, paprika, and peanut butter this a filling and enjoyable. Furthermore, we've kept the carb count down in order to keep you on your keto diet.

SERVING SIZE:

This recipe yields 3 servings.

INGREDIENTS:

1 tbsp. rice vinegar

2 tsp. chili paste

1/4 tsp. cayenne pepper

2 tsp. sesame oil

1 tbsp. erythritol

1 tsp. garlic (minced)

1/4 tsp. paprika

1/3 yellow pepper

4 tbsp. soy sauce

1 lb. ground chicken

2 spring onions

3 tbsp. peanut butter

1/2 lime (juiced)

Directions:

1. Place pan on medium-high heat, and add sesame oil.

2. When hot, brown your chicken.

3. Add all other ingredients, except onion and yellow pepper, to the pan and mix well.

4. When everything is cooked all the way through, add your onion and pepper.

5. Continue to cook until onion is translucent.

6. Salt and pepper to taste and serve.

Nicely done, enjoy!

Nutritional information (per serving):

Calories: 390

Fat: 22g

Carbs: 3.5g

Protein: 34g

Bacon and Cheddar Mug Cake

The easy mug cake sure packs a punch! A hot bacon, cheddar, and chive cake that's delicious and only takes a few minutes!

SERVING SIZE:

This recipe yields 1 serving.

INGREDIENTS:

Base:

2 tbsp. almond flour

1 large egg

2 tbsp. butter

1/2 tsp. baking powder

Inner:

1 tbsp. white cheddar (shredded)

1 tbsp. chive (chopped)

1 tbsp. cheddar (shredded)

2 slices bacon

1/4 tsp. Mrs. Dash (table blend)

1 tbsp. almond flour

1 pinch salt

DIRECTIONS:

1. Mix all your base ingredients together. Stir well so there are no clumps.

2. Now chop your bacon (already cooked) and chives, and add these two along with all your innards ingredients together. Mix well.

3. Now mix everything together in a mug, and microwave on high for 70 seconds.

4. Lightly tap the mug against a plate and the cake will tumble out.

Serve it up! Add extra chives on top if you wish.

NUTRITIONAL INFORMATION (PER SERVING):

Calories: 570

Fat: 54g

Carbs: 6g

Protein: 25g

KETO INSIDE-OUT BURGER

Want to avoid the carbs in a burger? Then just toss 'em out! This inside out burger is absolutely delicious and features two patties forming the 'bun' stuffed with all your favorite burger toppings.

SERVING SIZE:

This Recipe yields 6 servings.

INGREDIENTS:

8 slices bacon (chopped)

2 tsp. garlic (minced)

28 oz. ground beef

2 tbsp. chives (chopped)

2 tsp. black pepper

1 tbsp. soy sauce

1 tsp. Worcestershire sauce

1 1/4 tsp. salt

1 tsp. onion powder

1/4 cup cheddar cheese

DIRECTIONS:

1. Heat up a cast iron skillet and cook your chopped bacon until nice and crispy. Remove to a paper towel once cooked and reserve the grease.

2. In a bowl, mix all of your spices, the ground beef, and 2/3 of the bacon. Mix completely.

3. Form about 9 patties.

4. Now toss about 2 tbsp. of the bacon fat back into the skillet.

5. Once hot and sizzling, add your patties and cook about 5 minutes.

6. Remove the patties from the pan and let them cool for about 5 minutes.

7. Serve them up with cheese, more bacon, and onion if you like. All your favorite burger toppings!

Enjoy!

NUTRITIONAL INFORMATION (PER SERVING):

Calories: 430

Fat: 35g

Carbs: 2g

Protein: 30g

SCRUMPTIOUS SUNDAY ROAST

Feeling ambitious for your weekend lunch? Then break out a beef rib roast and get it cooking in your slow cooker all morning, filling your house with a wonderful aroma in the process!

SERVING SIZE:

This recipe yields 8 servings.

INGREDIENTS:

1 tsp. garlic powder

2 tsp. salt

1 tsp. pepper

5 lbs. beef rib roast

DIRECTIONS:

1. Take your rib roast out of the fridge and let it come to room temperature for about an hour.

2. Pre heat your oven to 375°F.

3. Break out your roasting rack, or a casserole dish will work as well.

4. Give your roast a rub down with all your spices.

5. Place the roast in whatever oven safe dish you're using, and cook for 1 hour.

6. After 1 hour, turn off the oven, but **DO NOT** open the door. Let it sit in the turned off oven for another 3 hours. This will make your roast nice and tender.

7. About 45 minutes prior to serving, turn the oven back on to heat up the roast.

8. After removing from the oven, let the roast rest for about 15 minutes before slicing.

Serving with your favorite vegetables and enjoy!

NUTRITIONAL INFORMATION (PER SERVING):

Calories: 680

Fat: 45g

Carbs: 0.5g

Protein: 92g

CHICKEN STIR FRY WITH BACON

This quick stir fry features cheesy sausages amongst a pile of vegetables and swimming in a zesty sauce of pepper flakes and butter. Perfect for preparing on the weekend and taking to work throughout the week!

SERVING SIZE:

This recipe yields 3 servings.

INGREDIENTS:

2 tbsp. butter (salted)

1/2 tsp. pepper

2 tsp. garlic (minced)

1/2 tsp. red pepper flakes

1/2 cup parmesan cheese

3 cups broccoli florets

1/2 cup tomato sauce

3 cups spinach

1/4 cup red wine (merlot works well!)

1/2 tsp. salt

4 cheddar & bacon chicken sausages

DIRECTIONS:

1. Slice your sausage into whatever sizes you wish.

2. Heat a pan on high, and toss in your sausage. Also bring a separate pot of water to boiling.

3. Throw your broccoli into the boiling water. Cook for about 5 minutes or until it reaches your desired consistency.

4. Continue to stir your sausages as they cook, until they are uniformly brown.

5. Nudge your sausages to one side of the pan and then drop the butter onto the other side.

6. Drop your garlic into the butter and cook for 1 to 2 minutes.

7. Now stir everything in your pan together and add your broccoli as well.

8. Pour in the red wine and tomato sauce. Sprinkle the pepper flakes in as well.

9. Mix everything together. Add the spinach, salt, and pepper. Continue to stir as it cooks down.

10. Simmer for 10 minutes

You're all set, enjoy!

NUTRITIONAL INFORMATION (PER SERVING):

Calories: 450

Fat: 29g

Carbs: 8g

Protein: 36g

BEEFY STUFFED PEPPERS

The classic stuffed pepper with beef and bacon! Not a hassle to prepare and excellent for keeping in the fridge for future use.

SERVING SIZE:
This recipe yields 4 servings.

INGREDIENTS:
1 tsp. hot sauce

1 tbsp. garlic (minced)

1 tsp. liquid smoke

3 tbsp. olive oil

1 1/2 tsp. Worcestershire sauce

1 tbsp. soy sauce

2 tsp. oregano

1/2 tsp. black pepper

2 tbsp. ketchup (sugar free)

4 bell peppers

1 1/2 lbs. ground beef

4 slices bacon (thick cut)

DIRECTIONS:

1. Break out a Ziploc bag, and toss in your beef, spices, and oil. Seal the bag, and mix all the contents thoroughly.

2. Allow this bag to sit in the fridge for at least 3 hours.

3. Preheat your oven to 350°F, and bring a pot of salted water to a boil on the stove.

4. Blanch the peppers in the boiling water for 3 minutes, and then immediately remove and dry them.

5. Finely chop your bacon and give it a light fry, don't cook it all the way. Add this bacon to the beef mixture.

6. Now stuff the peppers with the bacon and beef mixture.

7. Bake the peppers for 55 minutes. If you have a meat thermometer, cook until the filling is at medium for beef.

8. Sprinkle some cheese on top, and broil until the cheese is bubbling.

Serve and enjoy!

NUTRITIONAL INFORMATION (PER SERVING):

Calories: 590

Fat: 42g

Carbs: 5g

Protein: 49g

CHEDDAR DRAPED MEATBALLS

What could make your classic meatballs even better? Wrap them in a cloak of cheddar cheese! These meatballs are prefect as the main event of your lunch, or an appetizer for a party.

SERVING SIZE:

This recipe yields 24 servings.

INGREDIENTS:

1 tsp. cumin

1 cup cheddar cheese

1 cup tomato sauce

1/3 pork rinds (crushed)

2 large eggs

1 tsp. chili powder

1 1/2 chorizo sausage

1 1/2 lbs. ground beef

1 tsp. salt

DIRECTIONS:

1. Preheat your oven to 350°F.

2. Break up your sausage and mix it with the ground beef. You want a fairly uniform mixture here.

3. Now add your pork rinds, spices, cheese, and eggs to the beef mixture. Combine well.

4. Form your meatballs and lay them on a foiled baking sheet.

5. Bake for about 35 minutes, or until fully cooked.

6. Drizzle the tomato sauce over the meatballs and serve.

Enjoy!

NUTRITIONAL INFORMATION (PER SERVING):

Calories: 113

Fat: 8g

Carbs: 1g

Protein: 10g

PEPPER JACK MEATBALLS

Another fantastic meatball recipe! Here we have pepper jack cheese, Italian sausage, and beef to keep the hunger at bay.

SERVING SIZE:

This recipe yields 11 servings / meatballs.

INGREDIENTS:

5 slices pepper jack cheese

1 tsp. oregano

2 large eggs

1/3 cup pork rinds (crushed)

1 cup alfredo sauce

1 tsp. Italian seasoning

1 1/2 hot Italian sausage.

1 1/2 lbs. ground beef

1 tsp. salt

DIRECTIONS:

1. Preheat your oven to 350°F.

2. Break up the sausage and mix with the beef.

3. Now add the eggs, pork rinds, and spices to the beef mixture. Mix well.

4. Grab about 2/3 of the meat you would need for each meatball and form into a semicircle.

5. Place the pepper jack cheese on top of the circle and then seal it up with the rest of the meat you need for that meatball.

6. Place the meatballs on a foiled baking sheet and bake for 40 minutes, or until completely cooked.

7. Drizzle with alfredo sauce and serve.

Enjoy!

NUTRITIONAL INFORMATION (PER SERVING):

Calories: 290

Fat: 20g

Carbs: 1.5g

Protein: 23g

Cheese Stuffed Hotdogs with Bacon

Give your hotdogs some character by stuffing them with cheese! Better yet, wrap them in bacon for good measure!

Serving Size:

This recipe yields 6 servings.

Ingredients:

12 slices bacon

1/2 tsp. garlic powder

1/2 tsp. onion powder

2 oz. cheddar cheese

6 hotdogs

salt and pepper to taste

DIRECTIONS:

1. Preheat your oven to 400°F.

2. Slit all of the hotdogs lengthwise and stuff with the cheese.

3. Wrap the hotdogs with 2 slices of bacon each. Use toothpicks to secure the bacon.

4. Season to taste, and bake for 35 to 40 minutes.

Don't forget to take out the toothpicks, and enjoy!

NUTRITIONAL INFORMATION (PER SERVING):

Calories: 382

Fat: 35g

Carbs: 0.5g

Protein: 17g

Bok Choy Salad With Tofu

Here we have an interesting twist on the same old lunch salad. Switch things up by using bok choy, a thick leafy green, and cooking your own tofu. The tofu will have to be prepared the night before, but it's an excellent and filling lunch!

SERVING SIZE:

This recipe yields 3 servings.

INGREDIENTS:

Tofu:

1 tbsp. water

1 tbsp. soy sauce

2 tsp. garlic (minced)

1 tbsp. red wine vinegar

1 tbsp. sesame oil

15 oz. firm tofu

1/2 lemon (juiced)

Salad:

1 stalk green onion

2 tbsp. soy sauce

3 tbsp. coconut oil

1 tbsp. sambal olek

2 tbsp. cilantro (chopped)

9 oz. bok choy

1 tbsp. peanut butter

1/2 lime (juiced)

7 drops liquid stevia

DIRECTIONS:

1. Press dry the tofu. This will take nearly 6 hours.

2. Combine all of the tofu marinade ingredients and stir well.

3. Chop the tofu into uniform cubes, and drop into a plastics bag along with the marinade.

4. Let the tofu marinade overnight.

5. Now preheat your oven to 350°F.

6. Place the tofu on a backing sheet (on top of parchment paper), and bake for 35 minutes.

7. While this is baking, mix all the salad ingredients (except the choy). Add the cilantro and spring onion, and mix well.

8. Chop up the bok choy to whatever size you wish and remove the tofu from the oven.

Assemble your salad and enjoy!

NUTRITIONAL INFORMATION (PER SERVING):

Calories: 440

Fat: 36g

Carbs: 6g

Protein: 26g

KETO FRIENDLY NASI LEMAK

Take an adventure for your lunch and cook up some nasi lemak! This dish consists of rice and chicken cooked in coconut milk and is certain to give you some lunchtime flair!

SERVING SIZE:
This recipe yields 2 servings.

INGREDIENTS:
Chicken:

1/4 tsp. turmeric powder

1/8 tsp. salt

1/2 tsp. lime juice

1/2 tsp. curry powder

1/2 tsp. coconut oil

2 chicken thighs (boneless)

Nasi Lemak:

1/2 small shallot

1/4 tsp. salt

3 slices ginger

3 tbsp. coconut milk

7 oz. riced cauliflower

4 slices cucumber

Fried Egg:

1 large egg

1/2 tbsp. butter (unsalted)

DIRECTIONS:

1. Squeeze the water out of your riced cauliflower.

2. Combine your lime juice, salt, turmeric powder, and curry powder. Marinade the chicken thighs with this.

3. Fry the chicken until fully cooked.

4. Heat a saucepan, and toss in ginger, shallot, and coconut milk. Bring to a boil.

5. Once this is boiling, add the cauliflower rice and stir.

6. Fry your egg separately.

7. Dish up your rice mixture and eggs. Serve with 2 slices of cucumber.

All set!

NUTRITIONAL INFORMATION (PER SERVING):

Calories: 502

Fat: 40g

Carbs; 7g

Protein: 29g

"Food, in the end, in our own tradition, is something holy. It's not about nutrients and calories. It's about sharing. It's about honesty. It's about identity."

-Louise Fresco

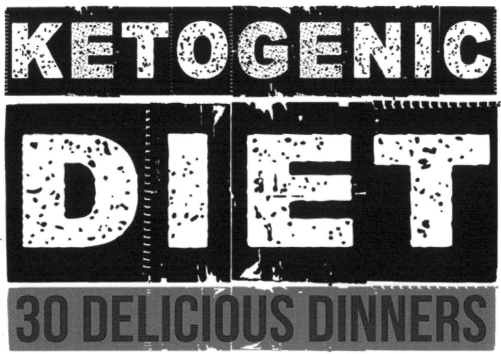

30 DELICIOUS DINNERS

1 MONTH OF LOW-CARB, HIGH-FAT WEIGHT LOSS MEALS

Recipes365

Nutty Salmon

This walnut crust salmon is sure to be a hit for dinner. Deliciously seasoned with mustard and dill, and it's packed with healthy fats to keep you on your diet.

Serving Size:

This recipe yields 2 servings.

Ingredients:

1/4 tsp. dill

1 tbsp. olive oil

1 tbsp. dijon mustard

2 salmon fillets (3 oz. each)

1/2 cup walnuts

2 tbsp. maple syrup (sugar free)

Salt and pepper to taste

DIRECTIONS:

1. Preheat your oven to 350°F.

2. Dump your syrup, mustard, and walnuts into a blender or food processor.

3. Pulse until you have a paste.

4. Heat a stovetop pan on high. Once hot, place your salmon skin side down in the pan.

5. Sear the salmon for about 3 minutes until the skin is crisp.

6. While searing the skin side, add the walnut paste to the side facing up.

7. Once done searing, transfer to the oven and bake for 7 to 8 minutes.

All done, enjoy!

NUTRITIONAL INFORMATION (PER SERVING):

Calories: 375

Fat: 44g

Carbs: 4g

Protein: 22g

CROCK POT OXTAILS

The crock pot is your best friend for dinner on a busy schedule. Just toss in the ingredients, forget for a few hours, and you've got a wonderful hot meal all ready. One such recipe is this crock pot oxtails dish.

SERVING SIZE:
This recipe yields 3 servings.

INGREDIENTS:
1 tsp. onion powder

3 tbsp. tomato paste

1 tsp. garlic (minced)

1 tbsp. fish sauce

2 tbsp. soy sauce

1 tsp. thyme (dried)

1/2 tsp. ginger (ground)

1/3 cup butter

2 lbs. oxtails

2 cups beef broth

1/2 tsp. guar gum

Salt and pepper to taste

DIRECTIONS:

1. Heat the beef broth on the stove, then add the fish sauce, tomato paste, soy sauce, and butter.

2. Once fully heated and mixed, add the mixture to a slow cooker and season with all your spices.

3. Add the oxtails to the slow cooker and mix well.

4. Set the slow cooker on low, and let cook for 7 hours.

5. Remove just the oxtails from the slow cooker, and set aside.

6. Now add the guar gum to what remains in the slow cooker, and use an immersion blender to pulse your mixture.

7. Now serve your oxtails and sauce along with your favorite side dish.

Enjoy!

NUTRITIONAL INFORMATION (PER SERVING):

Calories; 430

Fat: 30g

Carbs: 3.5g

Protein: 29g

KETO ASIAN STYLE SHORT RIBS

Give your standard ribs a delightful twist by throwing in some Asian style spice! The combination of ginger, soy sauce, and red pepper give this recipe a wonderful kick.

SERVING SIZE:

This recipe yields 4 servings.

INGREDIENTS:

Ribs and Marinade:

2 tbsp. rice vinegar

1/4 cup soy sauce

2 tbsp. fish sauce

6 large short ribs, flank cut (about 1.5 lbs.)

Asian Spice:

1/2 tsp. red pepper flakes

1/2 tsp. garlic (minced)

1/2 tsp. onion powder

1 tsp. ginger (ground)

1/2 tsp. sesame seed

1 tbsp. salt

1/4 tsp. cardamom

DIRECTIONS:

1. For the ribs, mix all of the marinade ingredients. Marinade the ribs for at least an hour.

2. Mix together all of the ingredients for the spice rub.

3. Remove the ribs from the marinade and rub with the spices from the previous step.

4. Heat your grill, and grill for approximately 5 minutes per side.

Bon appetite!

NUTRITIONAL INFORMATION (PER SERVING):

Calories: 415

Fat: 32g

Carbs: 1g

Protein: 30g

Easy Peezy Pizza

When you get home after a long day what can be better than a quick homemade pizza? With a crust of mostly egg and cheese, this keto pizza is delicious and customizable with all your favorite toppings!

SERVING SIZE:
This recipe yields 1 serving.

INGREDIENTS:
Crust:

1/2 tsp. Italian seasoning

1 tbsp. psyllium husk powder

2 large eggs

2 tsp. frying oil of choice

2 tbsp. parmesan cheese

Salt to taste

Toppings:

3 tbsp. tomato sauce

1 tbsp. basil (chopped)

1.5 oz. mozzarella cheese

DIRECTIONS:

1. Use a food processor, or blender, or immersion blender to combine all of the pizza crust ingredients.

2. Heat the oil in a frying pan, and add the crust mixture to the pan when hot. Spread into a circle.

3. Once the edges of the crust begin to brown, flip and cook for an additional 60 seconds.

4. Now top the crust with the cheese and tomato sauce, and broil for 2 minutes until the cheese begins to bubble.

Top with basil and enjoy!

NUTRITIONAL INFORMATION (PER SERVING):

Calories: 460

Fat: 36g

Carbs: 4g

Protein: 28g

SEARED RIBEYE

Ribeye, plain and simple. Just follow the recipe for searing and combine with your favorite fatty side dishes for a perfect keto friendly dinner!

SERVING SIZE:

This recipe yields 3 servings.

INGREDIENTS:

3 tbsp. bacon fat

salt and pepper to taste

2 medium ribeye steaks (about 1.25 lbs.)

DIRECTIONS:

1. Preheat your oven to 250°F.

2. Season the steaks with salt and pepper, then place on wire racks for baking.

3. Insert a meat thermometer into the streak.

4. Bake until the thermometer shows a temperature of 124°F.

5. Now heat a cast iron skillet on the stove and add your bacon grease. When very hot, sear your steaks for about 40 seconds per side.

All set, go eat!

NUTRITIONAL INFORMATION (PER SERVING):

Calories: 425

Fat: 32g

Carbs: 0g

Protein: 31g

KETO SALMON AND DILL SAUCE

The dill and salmon yields a delectable dish with the deep taste of salmon and a slight tangy hint of dill or sharp mustard. Give this salmon and dill sauce recipe a try and see for yourself!

SERVING SIZE:

This recipe yields 2 servings.

INGREDIENTS:

Salmon:

1 tbsp. duck fat

1 tsp. tarragon (dried)

1 tsp. dill weed (dried)

1 1/2 lbs. salmon fillet

Salt and pepper to taste.

Dill Sauce:

1/2 tsp. dill weed (dried)

1/4 cup heavy cream

1/2 tarragon (dried)

2 tbsp. butter

salt and pepper to taste

DIRECTIONS:

1. Slice your salmon so you have two fillets.

2. Season the meaty side with all of your salmon spices, and season the skin side with salt and pepper.

3. Heat a skillet over medium, and add the duck fat. When hot, add the salmon with the skin down.

4. Cook for about 5 minutes as the skin crisps. Once the skin is crispy, flip the salmon and reduce heat to low.

5. Cook for about 10 minutes, or until it is cooked to your liking.

6. When the salmon is removed from the pan, toss in all your spices for the dill sauce, and stir until they begin to turn brown.

7. Add the cream, and stir until hot.

Serve it up!

NUTRITIONAL INFORMATION (PER SERVING):

Calories: 465

Fat: 42g

Carbs: 2g

Protein: 23g

ORANGE DUCK BREAST

Give your duck some tang by mixing in some orange extract. A fun twist on the traditional duck roast, and sure to be an excellent dinner!

SERVING SIZE:
This recipe yields 1 serving.

INGREDIENTS:
1/2 tsp. orange extract

1 tbsp. swerve sweetener

1/4 tsp. sage

1 tbsp. heavy cream

2 tbsp. butter

1 cup spinach

6 oz. duck breast

DIRECTIONS:

1. Season the entire duck breast with salt and pepper, and score the top.

2. Heat a pan over medium-low, and add the butter and swerve. Cook until the butter begins to brown.

3. Add the orange extract and sage. Cook until the butter turns deep amber in color.

4. While this is cooking, set another pan on the stove and heat over medium-high. Add the duck breast to this pan.

5. Cook for a few minutes, or until the skin turns crisp. Then flip.

6. Now add the heavy cream to the butter mixture, and mix well.

7. When hot, pour the mixture over the duck breast, and cook for a further few minutes.

8. Toss the spinach into the pan and cook until wilted.

Enjoy!

NUTRITIONAL INFORMATION (PER SERVING)

Calories: 795

Fat: 72g

Carbs: 0g

Protein: 38g

Classic Ribeye

Steak, butter, and duck fat. That's all you need for this delicious ribeye along with some thyme for garnish. Try it with your favorite side dishes and enjoy!

SERVING SIZE:
This recipe yields 2 servings.

INGREDIENTS:
1 ribeye steak (~16 oz.)

1 tbsp. butter

1 tbsp. duck fat

1/2 tsp. thyme

Salt and pepper to taste

DIRECTIONS:

1. Preheat your oven to 400°F.

2. Place a cast iron skillet in the oven as it is warming.

3. Once the oven is up to temperature, remove the pan and place on the stove over medium heat.

4. Add the oil and steak to the pan. Sear the steak for about 2 minute

5. Turn over the steak, and bake in the oven for about 5 minutes.

6. Again remove the pan, and place over low heat on the stove.

7. Add your butter and thyme to the pan and mix with the oil.

8. Baste the steak for 4 minutes.

9. Let the steak rest for 5 minutes.

Put it into your face!

NUTRITIONAL INFORMATION (PER SERVING):

Calories: 748

Fat: 65g

Carbs: 0g

Protein: 39g

CHILI TURKEY LEGS

Give those turkey legs some spice by adding chili powder and cayenne pepper! This recipe is easy to follow and will provide you with a tasty and zippy end to your day.

SERVING SIZE:

This recipe yields 4 servings.

INGREDIENTS:

1/2 tsp. onion powder

1 tsp. liquid smoke

1/2 tsp. thyme (dried)

1/2 tsp. pepper

2 tsp. salt

1/4 tsp. cayenne pepper

1/2 tsp. garlic powder

1 tsp. Worcestershire sauce

1/2 tsp. ancho chili powder

2 turkey legs (about 1 lbs. each without bone)

2 tbsp. duck fat

DIRECTIONS:

1. Combine all dry spices in a bowl, then toss in the wet ingredients and mix thoroughly.

2. Dry the turkey legs with paper towel, and then rub in the seasoning.

3. Preheat oven to 350°F.

4. Heat a pan over medium-high, and add the duck fat.

5. When the oil begins to smoke, add the turkey legs and sear for 1 to 2 minutes per side.

6. Bake in the oven for 55 to 60 minutes or until completely cooked.

That's all folks!

NUTRITIONAL INFORMATION (PER SERVING):

Calories: 380

Fat: 21g

Carbs: 0.5g

Protein: 44g

Slow Roasted Pork Shoulder

A hearty roasted pork shoulder to round off the day. Simple preparation, keto friendly, and excellent for entertaining!

Serving Size:

This recipe yields 20 servings.

Ingredients:

1 tsp. black pepper

2 tsp. oregano

1 tsp. onion powder

1 tsp. garlic powder

3 1/2 tsp. salt

8 lbs. pork shoulder

DIRECTIONS:

1. Preheat oven to 250°F.

2. Dry the pork, then rub with the salt and spices.

3. Place the shoulder on a wire rack (a foiled baking sheet works too), and bake for 8 to 10 hours. Or until your meat thermometer reads 190°F.

4. Remove from the oven, and raise oven temperature to 500°F.

5. Cover the shoulder with foil and let rest for about 15 minutes.

6. Remove the foil from the shoulder, and roast in the oven for another 20 minutes, while rotating every 5 minutes.

7. Remove from oven and let rest for 20 minutes.

Serve this bad boy up!

Nutritional information (per serving):

Calories: 460

Fat: 35g

Carbs: 0.5g

Protein: 32g

Asian Spiced Chicken Thighs

Liven up your chicken thighs with some sriracha and red pepper! These zippy little devils provide an excellent laid-back dinner, or a quick snack during the day!

SERVING SIZE:

This recipe yields 4 servings.

INGREDIENTS:

1 tsp. ginger (minced)

1 tsp. garlic (minced)

1/4 tsp. xanthan gum

1 tsp. red pepper flakes

1 tbsp. ketchup (sugar free)

1 tbsp. olive oil

1 tbsp. rice wine vinegar

2 tsp. sriracha

4 cups spinach

6 chicken thighs (bone in and skin on)

Salt and pepper to taste

DIRECTIONS:

1. Preheat your oven to 425°F.

2. Dry your chicken and season the skin with salt and pepper.

3. Mix all of the sauce ingredients until a paste begins to form

4. Rub this sauce all over the chicken.

5. Lay the chicken on a wire rack

6. Bake for 45 to 50 minutes, or until the skin is crisp and slight charring appears.

7. Mix the spinach, some salt and pepper, red pepper flakes, and leftover chicken fat together, and serve alongside the baked chicken.

Enjoy!

NUTRITIONAL INFORMATION (PER SERVING):

Calories: 600

Fat: 52g

Carbs: 2g

Protein: 30g

BAKED POBLANO PEPPERS

Very similar to baked stuffed mushrooms, these peppers combine pork, mushrooms, cumin, and chili powder for a delicious dinner!

SERVING SIZE:
This recipe yields 4 servings.

INGREDIENTS:
7 baby bella mushrooms

1/2 onion

1/4 cup cilantro

4 poblano peppers

1 tsp. chili powder

1 tsp. cumin

1 tomato

1 tbsp. bacon fat

1 lb. ground pork

Salt and pepper to taste

DIRECTIONS:

1. Broil your poblano peppers in the oven for about 10 minutes. Flip or move every couple minutes to keep broiling consistent.

2. Heat a pan on the stove, and add the bacon fat. Once browned, add the cumin, chili, salt, and pepper.

3. Dice the onion and toss into the mixture, along with the garlic. Fully mix, and then add the mushrooms

4. Once the mushrooms are cooked, add the cilantro and chopped tomato.

5. Cook for a further 3 minutes.

6. Stuff the poblanos with the mixture and bake at 350°F for 9 to 10 minutes.

You're all done!

NUTRITIONAL INFORMATION (PER SERVING):

Calories: 365

Fat: 28g

Carbs: 6g

Protein: 22g

Coconut Shrimp

Shrimp with a tropical flair! Coconut crusted with a fruity apricot sauce, this keto recipe will fill you up for dinner and also keep those sweet cravings in check.

Serving Size:

This recipe yields 3 servings.

Ingredients:

Shrimp:

1 cup coconut flakes (unsweetened)

2 large egg whites

1 lb. shrimp (peeled and deveined)

2 tbsp. coconut flour

Sauce:

1 tbsp. lime juice

1 1/2 tbsp. rive wine vinegar

1 medium red chili (diced)

1/2 apricot preserves (sugar free)

1/4 tsp. red pepper flakes

DIRECTIONS:

1. Preheat your oven to 400°F

2. Beat the egg whites until soft peaks form.

3. Dip the shrimp in the coconut flour, then dip in the egg whites, then dip in the coconut flakes.

4. Lay the dipped shrimp on a greased baking sheet.

5. Bake the shrimp for 15 minutes

6. Finish them off with a 3 to 5 minute broil to give them some browning.

7. Combine all of the ingredients for the sauce and mix well.

Serve them up and enjoy!

NUTRITIONAL INFORMATION (PER SERVING):

Calories: 395

Fat: 22g

Carbs: 7g

Protein: 37g

SLOW COOKED LAMB

Break out that slow cooker for this fantastic leg of lamb stuffed with savory herbs. Get it prepared in just a few minutes and let the cooker do the rest!

SERVING SIZE:

This recipe yields 6 servings

INGREDIENTS:

3/4 tsp. rosemary (dried)

6 leaves mint

1 tbsp. maple syrup

2 tbsp. whole grain mustard

3/4 tsp. garlic

1/4 cup olive oil

2 lbs. leg of lamb

Salt and pepper to taste

4 sprigs thyme

DIRECTIONS:

1. Cut three slits across the top of the lamb.

2. Heat a slow cooker to low, and rub the lamb with olive oil, syrup, mustard, salt, and pepper.

3. Stuff each slit on the lamb with garlic and rosemary

4. Add to the slow cooker and leave for 7 hours.

5. Add thyme and mint to slow cooker and leave for an additional hour.

Enjoy!

NUTRITIONAL INFORMATION (PER SERVING):

Calories: 415

Fat: 35g

Carbs: 0.5g

Protein: 27g

CHICKEN WITH PAPRIKA

This keto chicken recipe combines sweet and spicy in the form of maple syrup and paprika. Cook this savory chicken in its sauce then drizzle right before serving.

SERVING SIZE:

This recipe yields 4 servings.

INGREDIENTS:

2 tbsp. Spanish smoked paprika

3 tbsp. olive oil

1 tbsp. maple syrup

2 tbsp. lemon juice

2 tsp. garlic (minced)

4 chicken breasts (boneless and skinless)

Salt and pepper to taste

DIRECTIONS:

1. Preheat your oven to 350°F.

2. Cut the chicken into chunks and season with the salt and pepper.

3. Combine all other ingredients separately to make the sauce.

4. Add about 1/3 of the sauce to your baking casserole dish or pan. Lay chicken on top of sauce.

5. Drizzle the rest of the sauce over the chicken.

6. Bake for 30 to 35 minutes, and then broil for a further 5 minutes.

Serve!

NUTRITIONAL INFORMATION (PER SERVING):

Calories: 275

Fat: 13.5g

Carbs: 2.5g

Protein: 36.5g

CURRIED CHICKEN THIGHS

A straight forward, keto friendly method for whipping up some curried chicken. Easy to cook and excellent for those tired weeknights!

SERVING SIZE:

This recipe yields 8 servings.

INGREDIENTS:

1/2 tsp. chili powder

1/2 tsp. coriander (ground)

1/2 tsp. cinnamon (ground)

1/2 tsp. cayenne pepper

1/2 tsp. allspice

1/2 tsp. cardamom (ground)

1/4 tsp. ginger

1 tsp. cumin (ground)

1 tsp. paprika

1 tsp. garlic powder

2 tsp. yellow curry

8 chicken thighs (bone in and skin on)

1/4 cup olive oil

1 1/2 tsp. salt

DIRECTIONS:

1. Preheat oven to 425°F.

2. In a bowl, mix all of your spices together.

3. Line a baking sheet with foil, and place all the chicken on the foil.

4. Rub the olive oil and spices over the chicken.

5. Bake for 50 minutes are until completely cooked.

6. Cool for 5 to 8 minutes.

Go enjoy your evening!

NUTRITIONAL INFORMATION (PER SERVING):

Calories: 278

Fat: 20g

Carbs: 0.5g

Protein: 22g

APPLEWOOD PORK CHOPS

Give your pork chops a subtle hint of Applewood and delicious dinner is all yours! Combine with your favorite fatty side dish and you've an excellent keto meal right in front of you.

SERVING SIZE:

This recipe yields 4 servings.

INGREDIENTS:

1/2 tsp. garlic powder

1 tsp. grill mates Applewood rub

1/2 tsp. black pepper

1/2 tsp. Mrs. Dash (table blend)

1 tsp. salt

2 tbsp. olive oil

2 2tsp. hidden valley powdered ranch

4 pork chops (bone in)

DIRECTIONS:

1. Combine all of the spices and rub into the pork chops.

2. Heat a pan on medium, and add the olive oil.

3. When hot, add the pork chops and cover.

4. Cook for about 10 minutes and then flip the chops.

5. Cook for a further 5 minutes (covered).

6. Turn the heat up to high, and flip chops again. Keep the pan uncovered now.

7. Cook for 2 minutes, and then let rest for 4 minutes

Serve and enjoy!

NUTRITIONAL INFORMATION (PER SERVING):

Calories: 260

Fat: 13g

Carbs: 1.5g

Protein: 35g

CHICKEN STEW

Whether it's a chilly, rainy, or stormy day; good old fashioned chicken stew is an excellent choice for dinner. Warming and comforting, this recipe fits the bill with some extra zip from hot wing sauce.

SERVING SIZE:

This recipe yields 5 servings.

INGREDIENTS:

2 tsp. garlic (minced)

3 tbsp. butter

2 tsp. paprika

2 tsp. ranch seasoning

1 tsp. red pepper flakes

1 tsp. oregano

1/2 cup sliced tomatoes

1 1/2 tomato sauce

3 lbs. chicken thigh

1 green pepper

1/3 cup hot wing sauce

3 cups mushrooms

DIRECTIONS:

1. Finely slice your mushrooms and pepper.

2. Set your crock pot on high and add the thighs, tomato slices, garlic, spices, tomato sauce, and hot sauce.

3. Also toss in peppers and mix.

4. Let the mixture cook for 2 hours.

5. Now turn the pot to low, give the mix a stir, and cook for 4 to 5 hours.

6. Dump in 3 tbsp. of butter and give another stir.

7. Remove the lid, and cook for an hour.

Savor the glory!

NUTRITIONAL INFORMATION (PER SERVING):

Calories: 360

Fat: 22g

Carbs: 8g

Protein: 33g

ASIAN PORK CHOPS

Once again, give the 'old reliable' recipes an upgrade by including some Asian style spices. Here we have pork chops mixed with anise, soy sauce, and sesame oil to create a unique and enjoyable culinary experience.

SERVING SIZE:

This recipe yields 2 servings.

INGREDIENTS:

1/2 tbsp. sambal chili paste

1/2 tsp. five spice

1/2 tbsp. ketchup (sugar free)

1 stalk lemon grass

4 garlic cloves (halved)

1 tbsp. almond flour

1 tbsp. fish sauce

1/2 tsp. peppercorns

1 1/2 tsp. soy sauce

1 tsp. sesame oil

1 medium star anise

4 boneless pork chops

DIRECTIONS:

1. Pound the pork chops to 1/2 inch thickness

2. Grind the peppercorns and star anise to a fine powder.

3. Combine the pepper, anise, lemongrass, and garlic. Grind until a paste forms.

4. Marinade the chops with the paste

5. Let the chops marinate for about 2 hours at room temperature.

6. Heat a pan on high. Coat your pork chops with the almond flour.

7. Sear the chops in the pan. This should take about 1 to 2 minutes per side.

8. Once the pork is cooked, cut them into slices.

9. Mix the sambal and ketchup to create your sauce.

Enjoy your masterpiece!

NUTRITIONAL INFORMATION (PER SERVING):

Calories: 275

Fat: 10g

Carbs: 5g

Protein: 35g

PORTOBELLO BURGERS

The constant battle to avoid the carbs in bread can be draining. But you can still have a good old fashioned burger! Dive into this recipe with the twist of mushrooms for the buns.

SERVING SIZE:

This recipe yields 1 serving.

INGREDIENTS:

Bun:

1 tsp. oregano

1 clove garlic

1/2 tbsp. coconut oil

2 Portobello mushroom caps

1 pinch each of salt and pepper

Burger:

1 tsp. each of salt and pepper

6 oz. beef

1 tbsp. dijon mustard

1/4 cup cheddar cheese

DIRECTIONS:

1. Preheat a griddle on high

2. In a container, combine the oil and spices for the bun

3. Scrape out the insides of the mushrooms, and marinate in the oil and spices

4. In a separate bowl, combine the meat, salt, pepper, cheese, and mustard.

5. Use your hands to form your burger patties.

6. Now add your mushrooms to the griddle and cook about 8 minutes.

7. Remove the mushrooms and toss the patties on. Cook about 5 minutes per side.

8. Assemble your burger with whatever toppings you like.

That's it!

NUTRITIONAL INFORMATION (PER SERVING):

Calories: 730

Fat: 46g

Carbs: 5g

Protein: 62g

BBQ Chicken Pizza

Slash the carbs in your pizza by making your own crust out of eggs and cheese! This recipe for BBQ chicken pizza will guide you through the quick and painless process of making your own pizza crust, along with some delectable toppings.

Serving Size:
This recipe yields 4 servings.

Ingredients:
Crust:

1 1/2 tsp. Italian seasoning

6 tbsp. parmesan cheese

3 tbsp. psyllium husk powder

6 large eggs

salt and pepper to taste

Toppings:

1 tbsp. mayonnaise

4 tbsp. tomato sauce

6 oz. rotisserie chicken (shredded)

4 tbsp. BBQ sauce

4 oz. cheddar cheese

DIRECTIONS:

1. Pre heat your oven to 425°F.

2. Combine all ingredients for the crust in a blender and pulse until thick. An immersion blender will serve this purpose as well.

3. Now spread the dough into a circle on a baking sheet or oven stone. Be sure you grease the surface first.

4. Bake for 10 minutes.

5. Flip the crust over, and pile up your toppings.

6. Broil for a further 10 minutes.

Enjoy, you deserve it.

NUTRITIONAL INFORMATION (PER SERVING):

Calories: 355

Fat: 25g

Carbs: 3g

Protein: 25g

CHEESE STUFFED BURGER

Imagine taking a bit from a juicy burger, and suddenly, there's cheese! The cheese stuffed burger, or the Juicy Lucy, is sure to be a grill or dinnertime favorite.

SERVING SIZE:

This recipe yields 2 servings / burgers.

INGREDIENTS:

1 oz. mozzarella cheese

1/2 tsp. pepper

1 tsp salt

2 oz. cheddar cheese

1 tsp. Cajun seasoning

1 tbsp. butter

2 slices bacon (cooked)

8 oz. ground beef

DIRECTIONS:

1. Use your hands to work all the spices into the beef.

2. Form your patties with the mozzarella cheese stuffed inside

3. Heat a pan on the stove and add 1 tbsp. of butter. When hot, add burger to the pan and cover.

4. Cook 2 to 3 minutes, flip, and sprinkle cheese on top. Cover again and cook to taste.

5. Feel fresh to recharge the butter in between burgers if you wish.

6. Chop your bacon and top the burgers.

Voila, ready to go!

NUTRITIONAL INFORMATION (PER SERVING):

Calories: 612

Fat: 50g

Carbs: 2g

Protein: 32g

TATER TOT STYLE NACHOS

What happens when you combine two cheesy side dishes? You get one amazingly delicious dinner course! This recipe for tater tot nachos tastes just as good as it sounds.

SERVING SIZE:

This recipe yields 2 servings.

INGREDIENTS:

6 oz. ground beef (cooked)

2 tbsp. sour cream

6 black olives

1 tbsp. salsa

1/2 jalapeno (sliced)

2 oz. cheddar cheese

2 tater tots (preferably homemade)

DIRECTIONS:

1. In a small cast iron skillet (or casserole dish) place 10 tots as the base layer.

2. Now add half of your beef and cheddar cheese. Repeat this stack-up again until you use all your ingredients.

3. Broil the dish for about 5 minutes until the cheese is fully melted and bubbly.

4. Serve with the black olives, sour cream, and jalapenos.

Enjoy!

NUTRITIONAL INFORMATION (PER SERVING):

Calories: 635

Fat: 53g

Carbs: 6g

Protein: 30g

CHIPOTLE CHICKEN WINGS WITH BLACKBERRY JAM

Game day for your favorite team? Have to bring food to a get together? Then whip up these tasty chipotle style chicken wings! Great for sharing or keep them all to yourself, and the blackberry jam in the next recipe makes the perfect side.

SERVING SIZE:

This recipe yields 5 servings

INGREDIENTS:

1/2 cup chipotle jam with blackberries (see next recipe)

1/2 cup water

3 lbs. chicken wings (~20)

Salt and pepper to taste

DIRECTIONS:

1. Combine the jam and water in a bowl using a fork or whisk to make sure everything is well mixed.

2. In a plastic bag, add all of the chicken, about 2/3s of the jam, salt, and pepper to taste. Make sure everything is well combined and leave to marinate for at least an hour.

3. Preheat oven to 400°F.

4. Lay the chicken on a greased baking sheet, and back for 15 minutes.

5. Flip the chicken, crank the temperature to 425°F, spread the remaining sauce over top, and back for another 25 to 30 minutes.

Eat as is or add the next recipe in.

NUTRITIONAL INFORMATION (PER SERVING):

Calories: 500

Fat: 40g

Carbs: 1.5g

Protein: 35g

CHIPOTLE JAM WITH BLACKBERRY

The spicy and fruity combination in this chipotle style blackberry jam makes this sauce an excellent accompaniment for almost any meat. We recommend dishing it up with our recipe for chipotle chicken wings.

SERVING SIZE:

This recipe yields 10 servings / tablespoons.

INGREDIENTS:

8 drops liquid stevia

1/4 cup MCT oil

1/4 cup erythritol

1/4 tsp. guar gum

8 oz. blackberries

1 1/2 whole chipotle peppers

DIRECTIONS:

1. Heat a pan over low, and add the blackberries. Cook until they are soft and have released their juices.

2. Add everything except the oil and guar gum to the pan. Use a fork to crush the blackberries and mix well.

3. Now turn up the heat to medium, add the oil, and bring to a boil.

4. Once boiling, reduce heat and simmer for a good 8 minutes.

5. Add the guar gum, and mix completely. Using a colander, strain the mixture into a container.

Stick on the side of a dish or eat solo!

NUTRITIONAL INFORMATION (PER SERVING):

Calories: 50

Fat: 6g

Carbs: 1.5g

Protein: 0.5g

Jalapeno Soup

If you're ready to take a break from the standard savory soups and stews, then give this jalapeno soup a try! Creamy and full of chicken this recipe will satisfy your spicy side (especially if you keep the jalapeno seeds in!)

SERVING SIZE:

This recipe yields 6 servings.

INGREDIENTS:

1 tsp. cilantro (dried)

1 tsp. onion powder

1 tsp. Cajun seasoning

1 tbsp. chicken fat

3 jalapenos (diced)

3 cups chicken broth

4 slices bacon (cooked)

6 oz. cream cheese

4 oz. cheddar cheese

4 chicken thighs (deboned)

salt and pepper to taste

2 tsp. garlic (minced)

DIRECTIONS:

1. Preheat your oven to 400°F.

2. Rub the seasoning onto the chicken and bake for 50 to 55 minutes.

3. Heat a pan over medium-high and add the chicken fat. Once hot, add your chicken bones and fry them for 10 minute.

4. Toss in the garlic and jalapenos. Stir and cook for another 4 minutes.

5. Now pour in the broth and spices. Continue to simmer while the chicken bakes.

6. Remove the chicken skin from the thighs and the bones from the pot.

7. Use an immersion blender to puree the jalapenos and garlic. Shred the meat and add to the pot.

8. Simmer for a further 10 minutes

9. Add the cream cheese and cheddar cheese. Stir to fully incorporate and simmer for 10 more minutes.

Garnish with the bacon and enjoy!

NUTRITIONAL INFORMATION (PER SERVING):

Calories: 550

Fat: 43g

Carbs: 4g

Protein: 34g

Bacon Cheddar Soup

When is it not a good time for bacon and cheese? Yup, that's what we thought. So dive into this bacon cheddar soup with gusto and enjoy!

Serving Size:

This recipe yields 5 servings.

Ingredients:

1 tsp. garlic powder

1/2 tsp. celery seed

1 tsp. thyme (dried)

1 tsp. onion powder

3/4 cup heavy cream

1/2 tsp. cumin

3 cups chicken broth

4 tbsp. butter

1/2 lbs. bacon

8 oz. cheddar cheese

Salt and pepper to taste

4 jalapeno peppers (diced)

DIRECTIONS:

1. Chop up the bacon to 1 inch slices. Cook until crisp and save the fat.

2. Now dice your jalapenos and cook in the saved bacon fat.

3. Now toss the bacon fat (we're still using it!) into a pot, along with the butter, spices, and broth. Bring the pot to a boil.

4. Once boiling, reduce heat and simmer for 15 minutes.

5. Use a food processor or immersion blender to puree the mixture. Then add the cream and shredded cheese.

6. Stir everything together and keep simmering. Salt and pepper to taste.

7. Add jalapenos and bacon to the pot and simmer for a final 5 minutes.

Enjoy!

NUTRITIONAL INFORMATION (PER SERVING):

Calories: 520

Fat: 50g

Carbs: 4g

Protein: 20g

Keto Chicken Nuggets

Have a hankering for some fast food chicken nuggets? Then make your own keto version! This recipe will satisfy your craving while still keeping you firmly on the ketogenic diet.

Serving Size:

This recipe yields 4 servings.

Ingredients:

Nuggets:

1/4 tsp. paprika

1/4 tsp. salt

1/4 tsp pepper

1/8 tsp. onion powder

1/8 tsp. cayenne pepper

1/4 tsp. chili powder

1/8 tsp. garlic powder

zest from 1 lime

1/4 cup almond flour

1 large egg

24 oz. chicken thighs

1.5 oz. pork rinds

1/4 cup flax meal

Sauce:

1 tbsp. lime juice

1/8 tsp. cumin

1/4 tsp. garlic powder

1/2 tsp. red chili flakes

1/2 avocado

1/2 cup mayonnaise

DIRECTIONS:

1. Add all the ingredients for the crust to a food processor and pulse together.

2. Put the crumbs in a bowl.

3. Whisk the egg is in separate container.

4. Dip each piece of chicken in the eggs and then crumbles, and lay on a greased baking tray.

5. Heat the oven to 400°F, and back for 15 to 18 minutes.

6. Make the sauce by combining all of the sauce ingredients, and mixing well.

Feast!

NUTRITIONAL INFORMATION (PER SERVING):

Calories: 612

Fat: 49g

Carbs: 2g

Protein: 39g

PORK TACOS

Here's your keto version of the classic pork taco. Pepper, lettuce, and pork and flax seed tortillas; easy to put together and add any other toppings that you feel like!

SERVING SIZE:
This recipe yields 3 servings.

INGREDIENTS:
1/4 tsp. garlic powder

1/4 tsp. oregano

3/4 yellow pepper

1/4 tsp. onion powder

1 lbs. pork shoulder (cooked)

1 tbsp. olive oil

1/2 tsp. salt

1/2 tsp. chipotle powder

1 jalapeno pepper

1 cup romaine lettuce

6 thin flax tortillas

1/4 tsp. pepper

DIRECTIONS:

1. Chop your pork into cubes. You can also shred it if you wish.

2. Combine all spices and oil, and add to plastic bag.

3. Toss the pork into the plastic bag and marinade for at least 45 minutes.

4. Heat 1 tbsp. olive oil in a sauce pan set to high heat; chop the vegetables and add to pan.

5. When vegetables are done, cook the pork on high heat until completely done and crisp.

6. Assemble your tacos with the vegetables, lettuce, and pork

Enjoy!

NUTRITIONAL INFORMATION (PER SERVING):

Calories: 715

Fat: 68g

Carbs: 3.5g

Protein: 36g

CHICKEN DRESSED AS BACON

This chicken can't pull the wool over our eyes; even though it will look like one giant slab of bacon once you wrap your bacon slices around the outside, and then bake it in a remarkable lemon mustard sauce. Sounds good doesn't it?

SERVING SIZE:

This recipe yields 8 servings.

INGREDIENTS:

1 small lime

1 tbsp. grain mustard

1 medium lemon

10 strips bacon

3 lbs. whole chicken (gutted)

4 sprigs fresh thyme

Salt and pepper to taste

DIRECTIONS:

1. Preheat oven to 500°F.

2. Season the chicken with salt and pepper, and stuff with the lemon, lime, and thyme.

3. Season bacon with salt and pepper and wrap over the chicken any way you wish.

4. Add the chicken to a roasting pan, and bake for 15 minutes.

5. Lower temperature to 350°F, and bake for a further 45 minutes.

6. Take the chicken out of the pan and place in foil, and transfer the fat and juice to a stovetop pan.

7. Bring pan to a boil and add mustard. Mix well.

Serve with the sauce on the side!

NUTRITIONAL INFORMATION (PER SERVING):

Calories: 375

Fat: 30g

Carbs: 2g

Protein: 24g

"I like food. I like eating. And I don't want to deprive myself of good food."

-Sarah Michelle Gellar

30 DELIGHTFUL DESSERTS

1 MONTH OF LOW-CARB, HIGH-FAT WEIGHT LOSS MEALS

Recipes365

Coconut Bars

These keto no-bake bars are a breeze to make! Just mix everything together and let 'em chill in the fridge.

SERVING SIZE:

This recipe yields 8 servings.

INGREDIENTS:

1 tsp. cinnamon

1/4 cup butter (melted)

1/2 cup cashews

1/4 cup maple syrup (sugar free)

1 cup almond flour

1/4 cup shredded coconut

1 pinch salt

DIRECTIONS:

1. Add the almond flour and melted flour to a large bowl. Mix well.

2. Now (with dramatic flourish) toss in the salt, syrup, coconut, and cinnamon.

3. Roughly chop the cashews and toss into the mixture. Make sure everything is well combined.

4. Place parchment paper in a baking dish and evenly spread the coconut mixture.

Chill for at least 2 hours.

Slice and munch!

NUTRITIONAL INFORMATION (PER SERVING):

Calories: 185

Fat: 18g

Carbs: 4.5g

Protein: 4g

Pumpkin Ice Cream with Pecans

Ice cream isn't just for the carb carefree anymore! Try the delicious pumpkin, keto friendly, ice cream recipe made with cottage cheese!

SERVING SIZE:

This recipe yields 4 servings.

INGREDIENTS:

2 cups coconut milk

1/2 tsp. xanthan gum

20 drops liquid stevia

1/2 cup pumpkin puree

1/2 cup cottage cheese

1/3 cup erythritol

3 large egg yolks

1 tsp. maple extract

1/2 cup pecans (toasted and chopped)

2 tbsp. butter (Salted)

1 tsp. pumpkin spice

DIRECTIONS:

1. Heat a pan on the stove and toss in the butter and pecans.

2. Now blend the remaining ingredients in either a blender, food processor, or immersion blender.

3. Now add the blended mixture to your ice cream machine, along with the pecans and butter.

4. Follow the churning instructions on your ice cream maker.

Simple as that, go eat!

NUTRITIONAL INFORMATION (PER SERVING):

Calories: 245

Fat: 22g

Carbs: 4g

Protein: 7g

PUMPKIN BLONDIES

These wonderfully soft and fluffy blondies with almond flour, pumpkin, and coconut will be an excellent treat during the day. Or the perfect dish of goodies to bring to a party!

SERVING SIZE:
This recipe yields 12 servings.

INGREDIENTS:

1/2 cup pumpkin puree

1/8 tsp. pumpkin pie spice

1 tsp. maple extract

1/4 cup almond flour

1/2 cup erythritol

1 large egg

1/2 cup butter (softened)

1 tsp. cinnamon

2 tbsp. coconut flour

15 drops liquid stevia

1 oz. pecans (chopped)

DIRECTIONS:

1. Preheat the oven to 350°F.

2. Mix the erythritol, puree, egg, and butter with an electric mixer.

3. Add the flours, cinnamon, stevia, pumpkin pie spice, and maple extract. Run through with the electric mixer again.

4. Grease a brownie pan, preferably with coconut oil, and pour in the mixture.

5. Sprinkle the chopped pecans over top.

6. Bake for about 20 to 25 minutes, until the edges and top appear golden.

Yours to enjoy!

NUTRITIONAL INFORMATION (PER SERVING):

Calories: 110

Fat: 11g

Carbs: 1.5g

Protein: 2g

PEANUT BUTTER FUDGE

Peanut butter? Right here. Fudge? Roger. Dark chocolate? Look no further. This peanut butter fudge recipe is utterly delicious and a perfect dessert for the keto diet.

SERVING SIZE:

This recipe yields 8 servings.

INGREDIENTS:

Fudge:

1/2 cup peanut butter

1/4 cup butter (melted)

1/2 tsp. vanilla extract

1/4 cup heavy cream

1/4 cup erythritol

1/8 tsp xanthan gum

Crust:

1 tbsp. erythritol

1/4 cup butter (melted)

1 cup almond flour

1/2 tsp. cinnamon

1 pinch salt

Topping:

1/3 cup dark chocolate (chopped)

DIRECTIONS:

1. Preheat your oven to 400°F.

2. Combine all of the ingredients for the crust, and mix thoroughly.

3. When smooth, line a baking dish with parchment paper and press the mixture into the bottom.

4. Bake for 10 minutes, and let cool.

5. Blend all the fudge ingredients with a food processor or blender. Now spread the fudge over the baked crust.

6. Top with the chopped chocolate and chill overnight.

Savor the sweetness!

NUTRITIONAL INFORMATION (PER SERVING):

Calories: 302

Fat: 19.5g

Carbs: 4g

Protein: 5g

BUTTERED PECAN ICE CREAM

Yet another gloriously keto friendly ice cream version! Enjoy this mouthwatering combination of browned butter, coconut, and pecans!

SERVING SIZE:

This recipe yields 4 servings.

INGREDIENTS:

5 tbsp. butter

1/4 tsp. xanthan gum

1 1/2 cups coconut milk (unsweetened)

25 drops liquid stevia

1/4 cup heavy cream

1/4 cup pecans (crushed)

DIRECTIONS:

1. Heat a pan on low, and add the butter. Heat until the butter turns amber.

2. Toss in the stevia, pecans, and cream. Stir continuously until well combined.

3. Now mix in the gum and milk.

4. Pour into your ice cream maker and follow the churning instructions.

Enjoy!

NUTRITIONAL INFORMATION (PER SERVING):

Calories: 315

Fat: 35g

Carbs: 1.5g

Protein: 0.5g

KETO MUG CHURRO

Churros in mug form! The same wonderful combination of vanilla, nutmeg, and cinnamon; but all combined in a mug and ready in seconds!

SERVING SIZE:

This recipe yields 1 serving.

INGREDIENTS:

1/4 tsp cinnamon

1 tbsp. erythritol

1/4 tsp. vanilla

1/4 tsp. nutmeg

1/2 tsp. baking powder

7 drops stevia

1/8 tsp. ginger

4 tbsp. almond flour

1/8 tsp. allspice

2 tbsp. butter

1 egg

DIRECTIONS:

1. Add all ingredients to a mug and mix completely.

2. Microwave on high for 60 to 70 seconds.

3. Tap the mug against and plate and the cake will fall out.

Into your face they go!

Nutritional information (per serving):

Calories: 435

Fat: 43g

Carbs: 5g

Protein: 11g

BUTTERSCOTCH ICE CREAM

Mmm butterscotch ice cream. Creamy, succulent, and keto friendly. With a dash of vodka for an added kick!

SERVING SIZE:

This recipe yields 3 servings.

INGREDIENTS:

3 tbsp. butter (browned)

25 drops liquid stevia

1/4 cup heavy cream

1/2 tsp. xanthan gum

2 tbsp. vodka

2 tsp. butterscotch flavoring

2 tbsp. erythritol

1/4 cup sour cream

1 cup coconut milk

1 tsp. sea salt

DIRECTIONS:

1. If not already done, brown your butter on low heat.

2. Blend all of the ingredients with a food processor, blender, or immersion blender.

3. Pour the mixture into your ice cream maker and follow instructions.

Enjoy!

NUTRITIONAL INFORMATION (PER SERVING):

Calories: 250

Fat: 23g

Carbs: 2.5g

Protein: 1g

MOCHA ICE CREAM

Give your ice cream a little dash of coffee to develop a deep mocha flavor; and combined with coconut milk and cocoa this ice cream is a winner.

SERVING SIZE:

This recipe yields 2 servings.

INGREDIENTS:

2 tbsp. erythritol

15 drops liquid stevia

1 tbsp. instant coffee

1 cup coconut milk

1/4 cup heavy cream

2 tbsp. cocoa powder

1/4 tsp. xanthan gum

DIRECTIONS:

1. Thoroughly blend all ingredients, except for the gum, in a blender or food processor.

2. Blend on lowest setting and slowly add the xanthan gum.

3. Pour the mixture into your ice cream machine and follow manufacturer's instructions.

Eat to your heart's content.

NUTRITIONAL INFORMATION (PER SERVING):

Calories: 143

Fat: 15.5g

Carbs: 2g

Protein: 1.5g

COCONUTTY CHOCOLATE MACAROONS

The combination of chocolate and coconut is a tried and true dessert favorite. Try our coconutty chocolate macaroons and find out for yourself!

SERVING SIZE:

This recipe yields 20 servings.

INGREDIENTS:

1/3 cup coconut (shredded and unsweetened)

3 tbsp. coconut flour

1/4 cup coconut oil

1 tsp. vanilla extract

1/2 tsp. baking powder

1 cup almond flour

2 large eggs

1/3 cup erythritol

1/4 tsp. salt

1/4 cup cocoa powder

DIRECTIONS:

1. Preheat your oven to 350°F.

2. Thoroughly mix all dry ingredients.

3. Now slowly add all the wet ingredients, while stirring continuously.

4. Use your hand to roll out the balls and place on a greased baking sheet.

5. Bake for 15 to 20 minutes

Share the love!

NUTRITIONAL INFORMATION (PER SERVING):

Calories: 75

Fat: 7g

Carbs: 1.5g

Protein: 2.5g

KETO COOKIE BUTTER

Keto cookie butter? Oh yes, it does exist. Oh recipe is perfect for spreading on bread, or other desserts, or eating by the spoonful!

SERVING SIZE:

This recipe is good for 16 servings.

INGREDIENTS:

2 tbsp. butter

1/8 tsp. nutmeg

1 tsp. vanilla

2 tbsp. heavy cream

1/8 tsp. cloves

1/4 tsp. ginger

1/4 tsp cinnamon

2 tbsp. swerve sweetener

1 cup macadamias

3/4 cup cashews

1 pinch salt

DIRECTIONS:

1. Add all the nuts to a food processor and pulse until smooth.

2. Heat a pan on medium and brown your butter. Mix in the swerve.

3. Now add the heavy cream and stir. Remove from heat and add to nut mixture in food processor.

4. Toss in the vanilla and all spices. Continue to process and make sure no lumps remain.

5. Process until you get your desired consistency.

Enjoy!

NUTRITIONAL INFORMATION (PER SERVING):

Calories: 112

Fat: 12g

1.5g

Protein: 2g

Peanut Butter Milkshake

This milkshake has only a few ingredients and will definitely help you satisfy that peanut butter craving. You can also tailor any of the ingredients until you get a shake that's your perfect fit! See our next recipe for strawberry milkshake to see how easy it is to customize this recipe.

SERVING SIZE:
This recipe yields 1 serving.

INGREDIENTS:
2 tbsp. Sugar free caramel syrup (such as SF Torani)

7 ice cubes

1 tbsp. MCT oil

1/4 tsp. xanthan gum

1 cup coconut milk

2 tbsp. peanut butter

DIRECTIONS:

1. Toss all of your ingredients into a blender, and blend until you get your desired consistency.

2. You can tailor the amount of ingredients until you get the taste and consistency you want.

Simple as that, really!

NUTRITIONAL INFORMATION (PER SERVING):

Calories: 365

Fat: 36g

Carbs: 5.5g

Protein: 7.5g

STRAWBERRY MILKSHAKE

Here's a variation on the peanut butter milkshake. Same base ingredients of coconut milk, MCT oil, and xanthan gum for the base, but you can always tailor your flavoring!

SERVING SIZE:

This recipe yields 1 serving:

INGREDIENTS:

2 tbsp. Sugar free strawberry syrup (such as SF Torani)

7 ice cubes

1 tbsp. MCT oil

1/4 tsp. xanthan gum

3/4 cup coconut milk

1/4 cup heavy cream

DIRECTIONS:

1. Toss all of your ingredients into a blender, and blend until you get your desired consistency.

2. You can tailor the amount of ingredients until you get the taste and consistency you want.

Enjoy!

Nutritional information (per serving):

Calories: 375

Fat: 42g

Carbs: 2.5g

Protein: 0g

Chunky Chocolate Ice Cream

The classic chocolate chunk ice cream, but keto friendly! Perfect for those warm evenings with avocados for added creaminess!

Serving Size:

This recipe yields 6 servings

Ingredients:

1/2 cup erythritol (powdered)

1/2 cup heavy cream

1/2 cup cocoa powder

1 cup coconut milk

2 tsp. vanilla extract

25 drops liquid stevia

6 squares baker's chocolate (unsweetened)

2 ripe avocados

DIRECTIONS:

1. Peel and remove the pits from your avocados. Add to a bowl along with the vanilla, milk, and cream.

2. Use an immersion blender until you have a uniform, creamy, mixture. A food processor would also work here.

3. Now toss in your cocoa powder, erythritol, and stevia.

4. Make sure everything is completely mixed then add the chopped chocolate to the bowl.

5. Refrigerate the mixture for at least 10 hours. Then add to ice cream maker and follow instructions.

Go get it!

NUTRITIONAL INFORMATION (PER SERVING):

Calories: 240

Fat: 22.5g

Carbs: 4g

Protein: 4g

CHIA SEED BLONDIES

Chia seeds make an excellent thickening agent for baking, and they're on the keto diet's side. Try out this blondie recipe using ground chia seeds and see for yourself!

SERVING SIZE:

This recipe yields 16 servings.

INGREDIENTS:

3 large eggs

1/4 cup erythritol (powdered)

3 tbsp. Sugar free salted caramel sauce (SF torani)

10 drops liquid stevia

1 tsp. baking powder

1/2 cup chia seeds (ground)

2 1/4 cups pecans (roasted)

3 tbsp. heavy cream

1 pinch salt

1/4 cup butter (melted)

DIRECTIONS:

1. Preheat oven to 350°F

2. Bake your pecans for about 10 minutes

3. Grind the erythritol and chia seeds in a food processor until a powder is formed.

4. Now add 2/3 of your pecans to a food processor (alone) and processor until a butter forms.

5. Toss in the stevia, salt, eggs, salt, and chia/erythritol. Mix well

6. Chop the remaining pecans, and add the rest of the ingredients to the batter. Mix well.

7. Place in a greased 9x9 baking pan and bake for 20 minutes.

Let cool and serve!

NUTRITIONAL INFORMATION (PER SERVING):

Calories: 175

Fat: 17g

Carbs: 1.5g

Protein: 4g

Coconut Mocha Mug Cake

Another quick, single serving, mug cake. Featuring a blend of coconut and mocha, this mug cake is a relaxing end to your day or a perfect midday snack!

Serving Size:

This recipe yields 1 serving.

Ingredients:

1 tbsp. cocoa powder

1/2 tsp. instant coffee

1 large egg

7 drops liquid stevia

1 tbsp. erythritol

1 tbsp. coconut milk

1 tbsp. shredded coconut (unsweetened)

2 tsp. coconut flour

2 tbsp. almond flour

1/2 tsp. baking powder

2 tbsp. butter

DIRECTIONS:

1. Add all ingredients to a mug and mix completely.

2. Microwave on high for 65 to 75 seconds.

3. Tap the mug against and plate and the cake will fall out.

Done!

NUTRITIONAL INFORMATION (PER SERVING):

Calories: 415

Fat: 39g

Carbs: 5g

Protein: 10.5g

GREENIE LATTE

Ginger! Allspice! Vanilla! And many more delicious ingredients make up this latte. Whip it up after dinner for a soothing evening and enjoy!

SERVING SIZE:

This recipe yields 2 servings.

INGREDIENTS:

1/2 tsp. cinnamon

3/4 cup coconut milk

1/4 tsp. allspice

1/4 tsp. ginger

2 tbsp. butter

1 cup strong brewed coffee

1/4 tsp. cardamom

2 tbsp. erythritol

1/2 tsp. vanilla extract

2 handfuls spinach

1/2 cup pumpkin puree

2 handfuls ice

10 drops liquid stevia

DIRECTIONS:

1. Add all of the ingredients to a blender or food processor and mix well.

2. Top with some extra cinnamon or homemade whipped cream if you like!

How easy was that?

NUTRITIONAL INFORMATION (PER SERVING):

Calories: 150

Fat: 14g

Carbs: 4g

Protein: 3g

WHISKEY VANILLA MUG CAKE

Mug cakes are an easy and fast antidote for a sweet tooth, and they can be keto friendly too! Try out this boozy version with some whiskey for an added boost!

SERVING SIZE:

This recipe yields 1 serving.

INGREDIENTS:

7 drops stevia

3 tbsp. almond flour

2 tbsp. butter

1 tbsp. erythritol

1 tbsp. whiskey

2 tsp. coconut flour

1/2 tsp. vanilla extract

1/2 tsp. baking powder

1 egg

DIRECTIONS:

1. Add all ingredients to a mug and mix completely.

2. Microwave on high for 80 to 90 seconds.

3. Tap the mug against and plate and the cake will fall out.

Enjoy!

NUTRITIONAL INFORMATION (PER SERVING):

Calories: 445

Fat: 41g

Carbs: 4.5g

Protein: 12.5g

Chocolate Peanut Butter Mug Cake

Yet another combination of peanut butter and chocolate! This time in the form of another mug cake. Made with almond flour and butter, this is a perfect dessert without torpedoing your keto diet!

SERVING SIZE:

This recipe yields 1 serving.

INGREDIENTS:

2 tbsp. almond flour

1/2 tsp. vanilla

1 tbsp. erythritol

10g dark chocolate

7 drops stevia

1 large egg

1 tbsp. peanut butter

1/2 tsp. baking powder

2 tbsp. butter

DIRECTIONS:

1. Add all ingredients to a mug and mix completely.

2. Microwave on high for 60 to 70 seconds.

3. Tap the mug against and plate and the cake will fall out.

Enjoy!

NUTRITIONAL INFORMATION (PER SERVING):

Calories: 490

Fat: 48g

Carbs: 4.5g

Protein: 13.5g

MAPLE MUG CAKE

Get the delicious taste of maple in your dessert with this mug cake. Wonderfully easy to make and you'll be enjoying it in no time!

SERVING SIZE:

This recipe yields 1 serving.

INGREDIENTS:

2 tbsp. almond flour

1/2 tsp. maple extract

2 tbsp. butter

2 tbsp. crushed pecans

7 drops stevia

1/2 tsp. baking powder

1/4 tsp. cinnamon

1 tbsp. erythritol

1 large egg

DIRECTIONS:

1. Add all ingredients to a mug and mix completely.

2. Microwave on high for 55 to 60 seconds.

3. Tap the mug against and plate and the cake will fall out.

Eat!

NUTRITIONAL INFORMATION (PER SERVING):

Calories: 435

Fat: 45g

Carbs: 3g

Protein: 10.5g

Chocolate Mug Cake

Classic chocolate brownie, in a mug, ready in seconds! Whip it up and enjoy this dessert staple.

Serving Size:

This recipe yields 2 servings.

Ingredients:

2 tsp. coconut flour

2 tbsp. butter (melted, salted)

2 tbsp. almond flour

1/2 tsp. baking powder

1 1/2 tbsp. erythritol

1/4 tsp. vanilla extract

1 large egg

2 tbsp. cocoa powder

DIRECTIONS:

1. Add all ingredients to a mug and mix completely.

2. Microwave on high for 65 to 70 seconds.

3. Tap the mug against and plate and the cake will fall out.

Simple, no?

Nutritional information (per serving):

Calories: 195

Fat: 20g

Carbs: 3g

Protein: 5.5g

KETO CHOCOLATE GANACHE

Here's a straightforward, keto style, chocolate ganache that can be used for any dessert! Try spreading it over some mug brownies, or coconut bars, or whatever chocolate goes with (which is basically everything).

SERVING SIZE:

This will be enough to cover the goodies we've made so far!

INGREDIENTS:

2 tbsp. heavy cream

1 1/2 oz. chocolate

DIRECTIONS:

1. Boil some water in a pot.

2. Place your chocolate and put it on top of the boiling water to melt it.

3. Once fully melted, add the cream and mix

Ahh, lovely!

NUTRITIONAL INFORMATION:

Calories: 323

Fat: 24g

Carbs: 5g

Protein: 3g

KETO CHOCOLATE

Ever wanted to make your own homemade chocolate? Well here you go! Just a few ingredients and it's all yours!

SERVING SIZE:

This recipe yields 24 servings.

INGREDIENTS:

2/3 cup LC-natural sweet white

1 cup expeller pressed coconut oil

1 cup cocoa powder

DIRECTIONS:

1. Add oil to bowl and melt over a hot pan of water (don't let the bowl touch the water).

2. Combine the cocoa and sweetener in a bowl and mix completely.

3. When oil is melted, add to cocoa mixture and mix thoroughly.

4. Cool, or chill in the fridge, until it reaches your desired consistency.

Enjoy!

NUTRITIONAL INFORMATION (PER SERVING):

Calories: 100

Fat: 9.5g

Carbs: 1g

Protein: 1g

Keto Hot Chocolate

Those cold and rainy evenings can be improved immeasurably by some hot chocolate. Here we have a keto save recipe that will warm you to the core!

SERVING SIZE:

This recipe yields 2 servings.

INGREDIENTS:

1/2 tsp. vanilla extract

2 tbsp. heavy cream

1 tsp. instant coffee

1 tbsp. Splenda

1/2 tsp. cinnamon

2 tbsp. cocoa powder (unsweetened)

1 1/2 cups coconut milk (unsweetened)

DIRECTIONS:

1. Heat a pan on medium and add the heavy cream and milk.

2. When the mixture starts to steam, add the coffee and cinnamon. Mix well

3. Now add the cocoa powder, and mix again.

4. Toss in the Splenda and vanilla, stir again and make sure no lumps are forming.

5. Now turn up the heat to high, and stir constantly until a rolling boil develops.

6. Once it begins to boil, turn down the heat and keep stirring.

When cooled to your desired level, serve it up!

NUTRITIONAL INFORMATION (PER SERVING):

Calories: 105

Fat: 9.5g

Carbs: 3.5g

Protein: 1g

PEANUT BUTTER AND CHOCOLATE PUDDING

Oh, chocolate and peanut butter, why are you so amazing together? If you need any further proof that these two may just be the best combination ever for dessert, try this pudding!

SERVING SIZE:

This recipe yields 1 serving.

INGREDIENTS:

1 tsp. cocoa powder

1/4 tsp. allspice

2 tbsp. peanut butter

5 drops liquid stevia

1 tbsp. coconut oil

1 tbsp. heavy cream

DIRECTIONS:

1. Combine all of the ingredients in a cup or mug and stir completely, making sure there are no lumps.

2. Freeze for a couple hours.

Pull out of the freezer and dive in!

NUTRITIONAL INFORMATION:

Calories: 386

Fat: 8g

Carbs: 4.5g

Protein: 7.5g

MUSCLE CHOCOLATE CAKE

Want a little protein boost while still enjoying dessert? Then whip up this chocolate mug cake made with a scoop of protein powder!

SERVING SIZE:

This recipe yields 1 serving:

INGREDIENTS:

1 scoop protein powder

2 large eggs

1 tbsp. heavy cream

1 packet Splenda

DIRECTIONS:

1. Add all of the ingredients to a mug and mix completely.

2. Microwave for about 1 minute, check, and microwave longer if you wish.

Go for it!

NUTRITIONAL INFORMATION:

Calories: 310

Fat: 15.5g

Carbs: 4.5g

Protein: 37g

CHOCOLATE PEANUT BUTTER ICE CREAM

Yet another combination of peanut butter and chocolate. Try this unique ice cream recipe incorporating cottage cheese for creaminess and protein powder!

SERVING SIZE:
This recipe yields 2 servings.

INGREDIENTS:
6 drops Splenda

2 tbsp. peanut butter

1 cup cottage cheese

1 scoop protein powder

2 tbsp. heavy cream

DIRECTIONS:

1. Combine the cheese and Splenda in a food processor.

2. Toss in the peanut butter and cream. Blend well.

3. Keep blending until all the cheese curds are smooth.

4. Now add the protein powder and blend again.

5. Freeze for at least an hour and enjoy!

NUTRITIONAL INFORMATION (PER SERVING):

Calories: 335

Fat: 18.5g

Carbs: 6g

Protein: 30.5g

Keto Mug Brownie

Chocolate mug brownie, plain and simple. Whip it up in seconds, enjoy, and repeat as required!

SERVING SIZE:

This recipe yields 1 serving.

INGREDIENTS:

1 tsp. cocoa powder

1 pinch baking soda

1 tbsp. egg white (beaten)

1 tbsp. almond butter

1/8 tsp. vanilla extract

3 drops stevia

1 pinch salt

DIRECTIONS:

1. Add all ingredients to a mug and mix completely.

2. Microwave on high for 50 seconds.

3. Tap the mug against and plate and the cake will fall out.

Knock it back, you deserve it!

NUTRITIONAL INFORMATION (PER SERVING):

Calories: 104

Fat: 8.5g

Carbs: 3g

Protein: 5g

KETO WHITE CHOCOLATE BARK

This deliciously smooth white chocolate bark makes an excellent dessert to have on hand in the fridge, or for taking to an event.

SERVING SIZE:

This recipe yields 12 servings.

INGREDIENTS:

1/2 tsp. hemp seed powder

1/3 cup LC-Natural sweet white

2 oz. cacao butter

1 tsp. vanilla powder

1 tsp. pumpkin seeds (toasted)

1 pinch salt

DIRECTIONS:

1. Melt the butter in a bowl over hot water, and make sure the bowl doesn't touch the water.

2. Mix all ingredients with the butter once it is melted.

3. Pour the mixture into a greased baking dish.

4. All the mixture time to set and firm up.

5. Placing in the freezer will also help speed up the setting process.

Yum, enjoy!

NUTRITIONAL INFORMATION (PER SERVING):

Calories: 40

Fat: 2g

Carbs: 0g

Protein: 0g

CHAI MUG CAKE

Chai tea is renowned for its soothing properties. So why not bring that over to a dessert! Try this blend of relaxing spices combined in a delectable brownie.

SERVING SIZE:

This recipe yields 1 serving.

INGREDIENTS:

4 tbsp. almond flour

7 drops stevia

1/4 tsp. cloves

1/4 tsp. cinnamon

1/4 tsp. vanilla

1/2 tsp. baking powder

1 tbsp. erythritol

2 tbsp. butter

1/4 tsp. cardamom

1/4 tsp. ginger

1 large egg

DIRECTIONS:

1. Add all ingredients to a mug and mix completely.

2. Microwave on high for 65 to 70 seconds.

3. Tap the mug against and plate and the cake will fall out.

All done and ready to eat!

NUTRITIONAL INFORMATION (PER SERVING):

Calories: 440

Fat: 44g

Carbs: 3.5g

Protein: 12.5g

MACADAMIA COCONUT CUSTARD

Nutty macadamia custard made in coconut milk to give it fantastic taste! We recommend chilling in the fridge overnight, so plan ahead with this one!

SERVING SIZE:

This recipe yields 4 servings.

INGREDIENTS:

1/3 cup macadamia nut butter

1 tsp. liquid stevia

1/3 cup heavy cream

1/3 cup erythritol

1 tsp. vanilla extract

4 large eggs

1 cup coconut milk (unsweetened)

DIRECTIONS:

1. Preheat your oven to 325°F.

2. Combine all of your ingredients in a bowl. Whisk well to make sure everything is combined.

3. Pour about 1 inch of water into the bottom of a baking dish and place four ramekins in the dish (the water should come about halfway up the sides)

4. Fill the ramekins with your mixture.

5. Bake for about 40 minutes. A knife will come out of the center clean when the custard is cooked.

6. Cool for half an hour.

That's it, good to go!

NUTRITIONAL INFORMATION (PER SERVING):

Calories: 272

Fat: 26g

Carbs: 3g

Protein: 6g

"A crust eaten in peace is better than a banquet partaken in anxiety."

-Aesop

FREE BONUS GUIDE:
TOP 10 KETO DIET MISTAKES

We hope you enjoy making your way through the delicious meals contained in this cookbook.

To ensure you stay safe and maximize your progress be sure to pick up your free bonus guide below now to avoid the top 10 keto diet mistakes!

Visit www.litomedia.com/ketogenic-mistakes to get your free bonus guide!

LIKE THIS BOOK?

If you enjoyed the meals in this cookbook, please visit your Amazon order history to leave a review and let us know.

If you also downloaded the free bonus guide, you will know the value of community, so don't forget to share this book with a friend too!